Emma with xx Mai mas 2023

GW00578250

Advanced Praise

Meeting the Muse After Midlife

Cleverly disguised as a memoir, this is a wise, witty, and captivating exploration of aging and creativity. The former we all endure, the latter we may aspire towards, but Sally shows in luminous prose that endurance and aspiration are not the right words for us. Instead, celebration and openness to the wonder and artistry of our lives are the optimum ways to express who we are. This book is like a masterclass in empowerment. Plus it's downright fun to read!

—**David Spangler**, author of *Apprenticed to Spirit*

Let Sally Jean Fox be your wise and funny guide on the path to becoming a passionate elder. Her memoir about meeting the muse after sixty is a paean to vulnerability, creativity and love, and how to remain fully human as time brings her inevitable changes. Beautifully done.

—**Mark Matousek**, Author of *Lessons From an American Stoic: How Emerson Can Change Your Life*

Sally Jean Fox is an inspiring storyteller, demonstrating how humor, joy, and creative expression are everyone's birthright, inspiring the voice of Truth within. Meeting the Muse After Midlife transforms our way of life from an acquiescent, linear struggle, into a multifaceted experience. Empowered by faith, courage and compassion, she calls us to live a life of true purpose, passion and possibility, beyond the myths of retirement and ageism. Meeting the Muse after Midlife will release new freedoms within you, offering a refreshing new perspective on what it means to grow older.

—**Chloe Goodchild**, author of The Naked Voice, Transform Your Life through the Power of Sound"

Sally Fox's spiritual memoir, *Meeting the Muse After Midlife*, is both intensely personal and archetypal in its vivid depiction of the journey to awakening. Aging, Sally shows us, is not the diminishment we are led to believe, but rather, the opportunity to embrace all of life as a thing of beauty. This is a wonderful contribution to the growing library of conscious aging literature. Highly recommended.

—CAROL OSBORN, author of *The Making of an Old Soul*

We each possess a creative spirit, but few of us recognize it, and even fewer still live in ways to give it wings—especially after midlife. Sally Fox's wise, funny book *Meeting the Muse After Midlife* shows us by example that aging is less about cognitive decline than about creative incline, if not creative flight. It's never too late to find your way. Let Sally Fox's story be your inspiring guide.

—JEFFREY DAVIS, author of *TRACKING WONDER: Reclaiming a Life of Meaning & Possibility in a World Obsessed with Productivity*

Sally does an incredible job of conveying the emotions and reflections many of us feel as we move into the third chapter of life. With a powerful, authentic voice, she shares the contradictions, hopes, and joys that come with life after fifty, offering the possibility that life becomes richer when we see it in terms of "both/and."

—MARGARET SEIDLER, author of *Power Surge*

Some books give rules, others examples, but the best weave tales, for only they can hold the truth. We enter Sally's stories as strangers, but, in them, we soon find friends. Their secrets we recognize, for they are our own. Sally's stories beckon us. She inspires us to remember our own true life and the pathway home.

—RICHARD OWEN GEER, director and author of *Story Bridge.*

Meeting the Muse is a joyride. There are struggles, and there is grief, but all along the way, the Muse is there, whispering: "Now paint. Now write. Now dance and sing." And why would you not, when life is so short and so precious?

—ANN HEDREEN, author of *Her Beautiful Brain*

Sally Fox masterfully guides her readers with honesty and love toward an understanding of the mysterious way that our material and spiritual worlds shape one another. Her love of creativity inspires us all to get curious about our own life journey.

—HEATHER WILLIAMS, author of *Drawing as a Sacred Activity*

We can reflect and recognize our own stories as Sally shows how she has lived with the polarities of aging—being humble while self-affirming and owning vulnerabilities while making peace with them. She invites us to see ourselves with appreciation for where we have been and who we are.

—BARRY JOHNSON, author of *Polarity Management*

Candid and courageous, *Meeting the Muse After Midlife* celebrates Sally's marvelous story of ripening into creativity. Trusting intuition and opening to the magic of inspiration, her testament invites readers to find their own way to heed the call to a mysterious emergent process that can lead to unexpected vitality and wonder.

—MARY OAK, author of *Heart's Oratorio*

There's a quiet revolution happening in the world: The second half and even the third act of life is taking on a whole new dimension. Sally Fox is a pioneer in this movement. A masterful storyteller, she takes us on a profound journey of awakening. We laugh and cry with her through trials and triumphs, then ultimately join her in claiming a creatively vibrant and spirit-filled life.

—DANA LYNNE ANDERSEN, author of *Art and Spirit: Creativity and the Transformation of Consciousness.*

Meeting
the Muse
After Midlife

Meeting the Muse After Midlife

A JOURNEY TO MEANING, CREATIVITY, AND JOY

SALLY JEAN FOX

rwl publishing

Copyrighted Material

Meeting the Muse After Midlife: A Journey to Meaning, Creativity, and Joy

Copyright © 2023 by Sally Jean Fox. All Rights Reserved.

No part of this publication may be reproduced, stored in a retrieval system or transmitted, in any form or by any means—electronic, mechanical, photocopying, recording or otherwise—without prior written permission from the publisher, except for the inclusion of brief quotations in a review.

For information about this title or to order other books and/or electronic media, contact the publisher:

RWL Publishing, Vashon, Washington
www.RWLPublishing.com
Info@RWLPublishing.com

ISBNs:
978-1-961785-00-7 (softcover)
978-1-961785-01-4 (eBook)

Library of congress number: 2023916036

Printed in the United States of America

Cover and Interior design: 1106 Design

Names and identifying characteristics have been changed to protect the privacy of certain individuals.

For my sister

Table of Contents

Prologue (Summer 1999)

I looked around at the 12 colleagues sitting on a motley collection of chairs in my living room, talking quietly to each other. I was hosting this circle of consultants, gathered for an afternoon of coffee, introductions, and potential collaborations—an idea proposed by a friend. After about ten minutes, it was time to interrupt the conversations and begin. I hesitated, took a breath, and said, "Welcome. I appreciate you all coming over. I can't wait to learn more about what everyone does. Why don't we begin by taking three minutes each to share?"

Except that I'm not sure what I do. I feel like I have a mouth stuffed with marshmallows every time I try to promote myself. A couple of years ago I could have said, "I run a university graduate program in management," and I thought that was going to be my calling for life. But I moved on. And now, as I'm approaching 50, I wonder if I've lost my direction.

"Why don't we each take a few minutes to share a bit about our-selves—who we are, what we do, and our hopes for the future." I turned to the man on my right, who was dressed with casual elegance in a blue crew sweater, polished loafers, and designer jeans. "John, would you mind starting?"

"I work with executives across the United States and Europe," he began.

Of course, you work with executives. They easily identify with you: tall, male, dark-haired, with streaks of gray around your temples. You've got authority before you even open your mouth.

"We produce value-added results for our clients. . . ."

Oh god, not those words—they make me gag—I can't even say them. Maybe that's my problem: I never sound business-y enough.

I relaxed as my friend Ellen started speaking. "I work with early childhood educators . . ." She always sounded so competent. But with that thought, the gremlin charged with comparing me to everyone else took hold.

Ellen's so organized when she conducts trainings. I'm more intuitive and random. I bet some of my clients would prefer the kind of structure she offers.

My mind drifted away as rays of light bounced off the black satin finish of the piano in the next room.

Music used to be such a part of my life. Why did I stop playing? Was it because of the back pain? Or . . . ?

I snapped to attention as another colleague began speaking. But my racing mind took over when I saw that I was up next and still didn't know how I would pitch my work.

How do I promote myself when my father's dying? Should I be honest and speak what's in my heart? "I'm a 48-year-old leadership development consultant and I don't know how to talk about what I offer because I feel like a mess. I'm headed into menopause, and every night is like a battleground. And I don't know how to even think about marketing when the one thing I care about is spending time with my dad."

When my time to talk came, the pull to sound credible took over. I opted for the traditional spiel: "I do leadership development consulting, helping managers understand themselves and communicate more effectively. I've got a PhD and an MBA, and I've been coaching adults for over 20 years."

Looking out at the polite stares on my colleagues' faces, I knew my words were dead on arrival. I sank back into my chair, embarrassed, politely listening to the others, counting the minutes until the meeting would be over and I could run downstairs and collapse on our meditation room floor.

I can't put on a show like this anymore. I want to stay connected to the deepest, truest part of myself—my Longing, the only place where I feel any peace. When I lie on the carpet crying or praying, I can feel my Longing guiding me from some inner aquifer of truth. When I'm in touch with it, I feel safe even if I'm full of holes. I don't have to worry about the future because I know I'm loved.

I thought about the shallow and scared part of me that was sitting in the circle trying to promote herself. Then, I thought about the part who knew to listen to the feelings of wisdom that sometimes surfaced from within. Occasionally, it would speak through a Muse-like voice, bringing my soul's perspective into my day-to-day life. I cherished those insights.

Listening to my colleagues in my living room, I heard the voice again. It whispered two words, almost demanding that I pay attention:

"There's more."

Introduction:
Welcome to the Quest

*W*elcome to a story about the quest for meaning after midlife, one that opened with those words, "*There's more.*" I have found my way, a step at a time, to a freedom and joy I never knew in my younger years. Without a roadmap, I made my path by walking it, gratefully guided by a deep Longing and a Muse who stepped in to help.

I hope my story will inspire you to trust what is calling you and give your heart to it— especially if you, like me, have passed the marker called "midlife." If you haven't yet reached 50, all the better; you don't have to wait to claim your creative freedom or discover what is yours to do. But aging can be a great mentor that forces us to learn. Sometimes, it offers lessons about loss, grief, and letting go. Other times, it bestows tremendous gifts, like the right to be ourselves and to let go of having to prove ourselves.

Aging taught me the importance of paradox, of looking at life through a "both/and" lens. Life, I discovered, can be *both* beautiful *and*, at times, brutal. It can be *both* joyful *and* tainted with grief; it can be *both* full of new freedoms *and* blessed with limitations. We can be *both* more creatively expressive *and* less agile.

But I'm getting ahead of myself. I didn't know any of this when I was 48 and melting down in my living room. I didn't know any of this before I was pulled to travel the road of creative expression. Back then, I thought the call was to reinvent my career. I didn't understand that was just the beginning. There would be so much *more*.

Oddly enough, my urge for change surfaced at a time when my life was going well. Although I struggled to promote myself, my consulting practice was solid, and I enjoyed working with my clients. I'd married a loving husband, bought a house, and achieved my lifelong dream of owning a horse. I had a reliable group of friends, many of whom were part of a supportive spiritual community. My 30-year-old self would have been ecstatic to see what I had done with my life. But, as I neared 50, doubts slipped in, and my previously steady ship started to rock.

I attributed my feelings to menopause, fatigue, and age. I'd rarely thought about aging through my thirties and forties; it was always at least 15 years in the future. But lately, the mirror was telling me otherwise. When I brushed my teeth, I still saw the young-ish face that friends claimed to recognize from grade school. Yet, I also saw an older face with blue circles under the eyes, wrinkles, and a gap emerging between its front teeth.

I'd anticipated some physical changes, but I hadn't anticipated the flock of doubts and questions that had also flown in, such as:

What do I want over the next decades?
What am I called to do in the second half of life?
Who is the person I am meant to be?

Here I was at almost 50, once again searching for a calling—a game I had thought was a young person's sport to be settled by age 35 at the latest. I wasn't sure if what had carried me through my early career was right for my next stage of life. I needed a guiding narrative that would help make sense of the years ahead. The stories I'd heard about aging in our culture—ones that were focused on "retirement" or "leisure living"—sounded boring or dreary. A few sounded unrealistic—at least for most of us. I really didn't care that some valiant elder

4

had backpacked across Mongolia or climbed Kilimanjaro when I had to gobble ibuprofen to make it through a three-mile walk. Other stories were plain delusional, like the idea that we didn't have to age at all or could avoid death altogether.

But the worst narrative, and the one underlying most of the others I heard, suggested that our last decades were nothing but a long off-ramp leading to death. It didn't make sense that God or some great Creator would have engineered human life so that we would spend our last third of life in purposeless decline.

None of these narratives, moreover, did anything to help me get out of bed on mornings when I was feeling stiff and exhausted. I'd read about research done by Dr. Becca Levy, who discovered that people with a positive view of aging lived an average of seven years longer than those with a negative view. Right there was the proof that we all needed to find a compelling story about aging that could marry realism with hope! I didn't want to sugarcoat the fact that the years ahead could bring loss, grief, and sorrow, but I wanted those years to have meaning.

A new mission emerged: I would create the storyline I wanted to live.

An Epiphany in the Air

Journey to Japan

I was overjoyed when a former client invited me to teach a leadership program in Japan. Marketing and self-promotion were never my forte, so opportunities like this made my heart sing—good money *and* meaningful work that I didn't have to chase down! After doing my happy dance, I put together a bid and eventually won a three-year contract to teach a binational group of managers. The job would include ten trips to Japan.

In my twenties, I had worked in international development. In recent years, however, all of my work had been in the U.S. Here at age 52, I was ecstatic to finally have another international assignment. Travel had always opened the door to different parts of myself, like the adventurer self I hadn't seen in a while. Maybe she could help me figure out what to do next.

I was hoping it might be a break from the emotional and physical roller coaster ride I'd been on since starting menopause. During the previous six months, a ninja team of hormones had invaded my internal control center and spun the dials. They'd introduced vast quantities of sweat, questions about the meaning of life, and dramatic mood swings. I could feel fine at 8 am and lament my fate by 3 pm. When a friend became an Amazon multi-millionaire, I couldn't control my jealousy-o-meter, and I melted into a pile of mush on the bed, regretting I'd never see such wealth. I tried to put a lid on such incredible pettiness and acknowledge my good fortune in life, but my hormone invaders just laughed.

Internal fires burned through me at night, and, one morning, when clients were about to arrive for a day-long leadership seminar at the house, I could barely get out of bed. I stumbled downstairs to the kitchen to make coffee for everyone and to guzzle the green tea I needed to rev my engines. Then, I headed back to the bedroom to finish dressing. Somehow, while I'd been fixing the coffee, the staircase I navigated multiple times a day had turned into a mountaintop I had to summit. I grasped the banister as if holding onto pitons and pulled myself up one step at a time. I caught my breath on the landing between the floors before making a final ascent to the top.

This is crazy. You shouldn't be mountaineering in your own house. Get help.

I finished dressing, applied a sweep of mascara and a single coat of lipstick, then ran downstairs to meet the first guest at the door. "Coffee's in the kitchen, and help yourself to treats. I'll be with you in a minute. I have to make a phone call." I darted to my office, shut the door, and dialed my doctor. "Could Dr. V please see me today?" I begged.

The receptionist slipped me into a 2 pm slot—right in the middle of my workday. But I took it, trusting that my teaching partner would cover for me. I must have looked distressed because when I asked her, she just said, "You go."

My doctor, a holistic MD with a scraggly gray ponytail and kind manner, greeted me and asked, "What's up?"

I described my situation, then said, "I think I might be perimenopausal."

He laughed. "Of course you are." He sent me off with a hug, a prescription for bioidentical hormones, and some hope. Thanks to the treatment, my night sweats subsided enough to let me sleep. But the doubts and questions didn't disappear.

Multiple trips to Japan sounded like the other prescription I needed. My energy picked up as I prepared for my first one in 2003. And, the moment I stepped off the plane, my adventurer self met me on the tarmac. Despite my fatigue from a 13-hour flight and a long wait at customs, I bounded into the lobby of Tokyo's Narita airport, enthralled by the carnival-like scene and the crowds rushing by me. Loudspeakers blared messages in Japanese and English. Restaurants, sushi bars, and convenience stores lured me with their food. Before boarding the bus to Tokyo, I stopped in one shop and surveyed an incredible assortment of rice dishes, pickled vegetables, tempura, and dinners packaged in elegant bento boxes. I grabbed one particularly colorful assortment, along with a can of green tea and a package of sweet crackers to nibble on during the two-hour ride into Tokyo. Soon, I was on the bus, thrilled to stare at a surrealistic skyline of highways, high-rises, and skyscrapers as dusk fell.

On that first trip, I was intimidated by the language and did little traveling on my own. But by my second trip, I found that I needed only a few words of Japanese to navigate Tokyo. I became braver and began taking subways and exploring the neighborhoods filled with pedestrians, neon lights, and a constant din. I stared at super-sized billboards featuring blond-haired Western models and kanji lettering.

Going to a department store felt like visiting an art gallery. Clothes were arranged by color and size, creating broad sweeps of purple, yellow, and green that looked like they'd been brushed across an artist's canvas. The sales staff hung garments carefully, measuring the spaces between each of the pieces to give them visibility and breathing room.

In the store's basement, sushi, sashimi, sweets, vegetables, and rice cakes lay in tempting refrigerated displays. I drooled at the dessert counter with its colorful rows of mochi balls, each holding yummy sweet bean paste inside. When I ordered two pieces, the clerk wrapped them in tissue paper and placed them in a white box tied with a ribbon. She made a slight bow as she presented them, like a gift, to me.

One Saturday, I woke up before dawn to visit Tokyo's Tsukiji Fish Market, home to the world's largest tuna auction. I shivered, standing on the cold cement floor in my running shoes, trying to avoid the puddles of water left by the hoses spraying the area. Thousand-pound tuna lay in rows like beached whales, their skins marked, awaiting the highest bidders. A fishmonger would periodically stab a frozen hulk with a long, sword-like knife and then pull out a slice of tender pink flesh to show its perfection to a potential customer.

When my need to warm up superseded my fascination, I headed to a simple stand where a vendor served me noodle broth with bok choy, chunks of tofu, and chives—the best bowl of soup I'd ever eaten. Following the lead of the Japanese customers, I slurped it down, enjoying the drops of hot liquid trickling down my chin.

At Tokyo's Shibuya Crossing, I stood mesmerized as thousands of commuters streamed across the intersection and toward the subway. Speakers pumped music to the crowd. Hawkers used bullhorns to promote their CDs, plastic purses, umbrellas, and the ubiquitous plastic and ceramic versions of the *maneki-neko*, the Japanese lucky cat. High above, a hundred-foot Jurassic dinosaur strode across a billboard like a refugee from an amusement park.

This loud, garish side of Tokyo, obsessed with pink Hello Kitty merchandise and huge-eyed anime characters, enchanted me. However, I was even more drawn to the traditional arts I saw displayed in the more understated shops. I would stand outside a window gawking at an antique handmade *chawan* (ceremonial tea bowl) worth thousands of dollars, despite its apparent rough surface and irregularity. I learned about *wabi-sabi*, the Japanese appreciation for impermanence and the imperfect perfection in both art and the natural world.

When I traveled to the countryside, the subdued elegance of the traditional houses with dark cypress wood, golden *tatami* (straw) mats and white *shoji* (paper) screens awed me. *Tokonoma* (display alcoves built into the walls) held the beautiful minimalist flower arrangements known as *ikebana*.

I visited Kyoto at the end of one of my work stints and found the beauty of the gardens to be like nothing I had seen. Even the fallen leaves in a temple garden looked like an artist's work. I saw more shades of green than I could imagine in the sea of bamboo, moss, spruce, cypress, pine, and camellia. The garden ponds and streams captivated me with their natural elegance, even though I knew that constructing them had required much human work. Colossal rocks in the Zen gardens drew me into silence and contemplation.

I couldn't get enough of the beauty I saw before me. In fact, at closing time, polite guards had to remind me to leave. *"Sumimasen,"* they finally said—"Excuse me." I wanted to beg for just a few more minutes but strolled slowly toward the exit, turning around frequently to take photos with my heart.

This place seemed like it was awakening something in me. Somehow, I sensed that my experiences in Japan were tied to my search, though I wasn't sure how.

Flying Home

*Beauty is what stirs your soul. Let it pull you
forward even when the path feels too dark.*
— ISABEL

*M*y eyes swelled with sadness as I boarded the plane after my last
teaching week in Japan. I was already missing the beauty, the
food, the people, and the fun I'd had with my Japanese clients. I nestled
into my seat and covered myself with a scratchy blanket to hide my tears.

Safe in my woolen cave, I surfaced only for the occasional beverage
or invitation to eat a lifeless chicken dinner. Where was the beautifully
designed bento box, the succulent sushi, the mouth-watering mochi, or
the ever-present green tea? Where in Seattle would I find anything like
the understated elegance of the Japanese gardens or the excitement of
Tokyo at night? When would I again slurp delicious homemade noodles
and let them trickle down my chin? Or savor the sweet smell of incense-
seasoned wood in the temples while bells rang in the background? Or
watch bamboo swaying in groves, each tree reaching toward the sky as
if in prayer?

I thought of my Japanese students and how respectful, observant,
and appreciative they'd been—so different than some managers I worked
with in the States. My colleagues in Tokyo had taught me as much as I
had taught them. I wondered if I'd ever again feel as stimulated teaching
as I had during this three-year contract.

I tried to think about everything I looked forward to in Seattle: my husband, horse, family, and friends, but a nagging question lingered:

If I like so much about my life back home, why am I feeling so heavy?

Then, I remembered the yoke of productivity and achievement awaiting me in Seattle, one I had carted around for many years. I had followed the rules for building a successful career in an achievement-oriented culture for two decades. I had chosen producing over playing, achieving over appreciating, and making sense over soaking in the sensual. Those choices had propelled my career, but they had also locked me into a way of life that, as I sat on the plane contemplating my return to it, felt constraining.

Since I had been self-employed full-time for nine years by that point, I had flexibility in scheduling my time and could ride my horse during the workday if I wanted to. But I always felt like I needed to make up for "time off" by staying in the office until late at night. I'd be at my desk at 10 pm answering "just a few more" emails. I'd read "one more" work-related book on a Sunday to put the finishing touches on a course. I routinely took my computer with me on vacation. I lived tethered to a list of what I needed to accomplish.

I'm tired of pushing and trying to be someone.

When would I take time to pause for pleasure and beauty as I'd done in Japan? Was I even capable of remembering to do that, much less prioritizing it? I can't imagine sitting for an hour soaking in the magic of a garden.

In Japan, every day had been an adventure, and I had been an artful explorer, curious and free.

Where will I find that freedom and joy?

Huddled under my airplane blanket, I felt a cloud of depression approaching, circling near the overhead bins. I knew it would be ready to dump its darkness upon me if I couldn't find what would bring me joy back in Seattle.

I need an answer, and I've got eleven hours on this plane to find it.

Usually, when I thought about the future, I enjoyed doing planning and visioning exercises. I was good at translating dreams into goals and action plans. Yet, as I sat in the plane facing my return to Seattle, such exercises felt too cerebral. I needed inspiration that would speak to my body and senses. I flashed through a list of sensual pleasures I enjoyed:

~ The touch of rabbit fur on my bare skin

~ The smell of lavender

~ Daffodils

~ The sound of the Brahms intermezzo I once played on my piano

As I imagined each item, I felt a deep hunger for beauty that I could feel through my senses. Working in "push mode" and trying always to do more had left little time for such delights. But in the Japanese gardens, my relationship with beauty had changed, and now it seemed to be calling.

For some women, creating beauty seemed to come to them naturally, whether they were setting a table, choosing earrings, decorating a mantle, or writing a poem. I had never been one of those women. But perhaps I was changing. And the relationship to beauty I was craving felt like more than a passive appreciation. I also wanted to create it.

I let my mind wander, interrupted only by overhead announcements to fasten my seat belt as the plane bounced through the turbulent air. I dreamed of colors and imagined soft clouds of pinks, purples, and blues. I imagined sitting on the floor surrounded by jars of red, gold, and green paint and dipping my fingers into them.

Color is beautiful, sensual, and fun—and, unlike so many pleasurable things, doesn't cost me any calories!

As I poured through a series of dream-like images, a word popped into my mind:

Peonies

As the image of the flowers flooded my body, I knew that I'd received a message. I inhaled and smelled a delicate fragrance coming from a flower that I'd never purchased or planted. I breathed again and pictured a bouquet of soft colors and velvety petals begging to be touched. Peonies seemed to be inviting me into a new world.

I want to know the magic of Beauty—and be able to feel it and express it.

I knew this was how my Longing spoke to me—with a sense of wholeness and "this is it" rightness I could trust. It was the kind of knowing that had flooded me 19 years earlier when I sat snuggled next to the fireplace with my new boyfriend. While we listened to crackling flames in my darkened living room, a voice surprised me by announcing, "He's the one." I had only known the man, Steve, less than five weeks, but eight months later, we were married. That voice and the knowing behind it led to 19 years of a happy and ever-deepening partnership.

As the "prepare for landing" announcement interrupted my reverie, I gathered my belongings and began picturing the happy face of the husband waiting for me. I exited the plane feeling energized and exhausted. I had no idea that the clue I'd been given would launch a quest that would continue over the next 20 years.

Digging In

First Steps on the Path

After the plane landed, I picked up my suitcase, passed through customs, and staggered toward the terminal exit. At 6 am, all was silent except for the whoosh of baggage carousels and the hum of quiet conversations among passengers.

Where were the crowds from the Tokyo airport? The sushi vendors? The dual-language announcements?

I entered the main airport lobby and scanned the crowd for an older man with blue eyes and a welcoming grin—likely to be wearing a soft plaid flannel shirt, faded jeans, and a baseball cap. Moments later, Steve caught my eye and walked toward me, beaming and waving. He opened his arms, and I fell into them, soaking up the musky scent that assured me I was home.

Back at our house, I nibbled on some toast and yogurt, then crashed into sleep, forcing myself to get up for the chicken, salad, and rice Steve had prepared. Although grateful for dinner, I still yearned for the taste of miso, sushi, sake, and soy.

I didn't share my in-flight epiphany, fearing that talking about it might dilute its power. It's one thing to hear the call to create and another to actually make something. On the plane, I had dreamed of a life replete with palettes of colors, textures, textiles, paper, brushes, a piano, a tambourine, and space to dance. I saw my hands squishing clay into forms, moving paints with my fingers, and plunking a keyboard. But with my legs back on the ground in Seattle, I needed to take action if I wanted to honor the gift of the *peonies* message. While it occurred to me that 55 might be late in life to be a beginner, I couldn't wait to explore what I might create.

I scoured our bookcases for my worn copy of Julia Cameron's *The Artist's Way*, the surest guide I knew for launching a more creative path. I began her practice of writing three "morning pages" a day but felt more drawn to her suggestion of taking a weekly solo expedition she called an "artist's date." The local art supply shop, which I'd never entered, jumped out as a place I'd love to visit.

On my date afternoon, I found the store's entrance off a back alley, under a local computer repair shop. I descended a concrete ramp and stepped into a wonderland of art materials. Looking up, I saw that someone had painted color swatches on the old basement ceiling, decorating a space that felt both a bit dilapidated and perfect for sparking creativity. I ambled down aisles of paints, markers, papers, and objects I didn't recognize. In the brushes section, I slid my hand along their sable and synthetic tops, letting the fibers tickle my palms. Oils, acrylics, and watercolor paints were given their own rows to strut their stuff, in gorgeous shades I'd never heard of. When I got to the markers, I opened and smelled several of the thick-pointed pens, relieved they didn't emit the awful bubble gum scents of my childhood "Mr. Marker" sets.

A young clerk with pink swatches in her hair saw me and asked, "Need any help?"

Yes, I wanted to say. How do people learn to do all this? How would I know which brush to use, and what is gouache—and, is it true that one can learn to draw?

Several 20-something art students walked by us on their way to the brush section. They seemed to know exactly what they wanted as they quickly filled their baskets.

I'm more of a stranger here than in a Japanese supermarket.

I mumbled to the clerk, "I'm fine, thank you," then headed to the back of the store where I'd been told I'd find rice papers.

Despite the dull overhead lights in the specialty paper section, the sheets glowed. Each piece was carefully hung on a wooden rack, looking beautiful enough to be a stand-alone wall decoration. I craved them all. I remembered how the Japanese used rice paper to wrap gifts, create lanterns, and build screens. I thought about buying several sheets, but then I remembered my artist's date guideline: I had a guilt-free budget of $20 to spend, and it didn't matter whether I needed or would ever use what I bought. An assortment of paper would cost too much. But I could get some other fun things, which I found down the aisle where pens and markers lived.

I took my stash to the cashier. It consisted of:

~ Two graphite pencils

~ An amber-colored eraser

~ A royal purple two-ended marker

~ A small pad of drawing paper

The cashier rang me up, and I floated home in a cloud of abundance.

That night, I was still craving papers like the ones I'd seen. At 8 pm, the art store was closed, so I checked out some online paper distributors. I saw translucent Japanese *washi* paper made from hemp, mulberry sheets specked with bark from Thailand, and elegant black rag papers from India with woven metallic gold threads. Then inspiration struck: I realized that, if I learned the art of Japanese paper wrapping, I'd have an excuse to use such papers—especially since Christmas was approaching. I picked out five large sheets with a variety of textures—nubby, rippled, seeded, and smooth—put them in my online cart, and tapped in my credit card number. I couldn't wait to stroke them when they arrived the following week.

Armed with an instruction book, I experimented. The Japanese use many materials beyond paper to wrap gifts, including fabric remnants, ribbons, straw, and objects from nature. Soon, I was scouring my dresser drawers for old scarves and walking our small Seattle house lot looking for dried grasses and short evergreen branches.

For someone like me, trained in the stick-on-a-bow-and-go school of American paper wrapping, I couldn't believe the time Japanese-style wrapping required. Despite my best efforts, my scarf wraps looked like potato sacks, and the corners of my paper wraps never laid flat. My first attempt to use a glue gun to stick pine cones on a package sent streams of clear hot plastic running down my shirt.

Despite my clumsiness, I presented my family with gifts wrapped in the Japanese style that Christmas. In addition to celebrating the holiday, I was celebrating my first steps on a new creative path.

Who Gets to Be Called Creative?

Creative expression is our birthright
and not a commodity to be measured!
—SJF, AGE 57

*S*hortly after the holidays, I met my friend Jeannie at our favorite Seattle café where we ordered lattes and enjoyed the sweet, yeasty fragrance of freshly baked breads and muffins. One of the luxuries of our shared status as self-employed consultants was having catch-up conversations at 9 am while other folks had to queue up for coffee then rush to work.

I had sped to our meeting, so I looked and felt a bit disheveled. Jeannie, however, looked elegant, even in her gym clothes. She could turn a hoodie into a fashion statement, especially when it was brightened with a coordinated scarf and earrings.

Oh well. At least my socks match.

Jeannie was dying to show me photos of her kitchen. She obviously had a designer's eye; the cabinets, windows, appliances, table, and floor all went together beautifully, and I told her so. I thought of my dining room, with its mélange of thrift store chairs and homey appearance.

I'll never have the affluence to do that kind of remodel. But who does? I wish I didn't compare myself so much. I'm incredibly lucky and grateful to have the life I have . . . and be with Steve. I'm on a different path, and I notice different things. But I love seeing how Jeannie lights up when she talks about her kitchen.

After she put her phone down, I began sharing my in-flight epiphany and describing my adventures in paper wrapping. As I bubbled on about what I might try next, she sighed and surprised me by interrupting my ramblings. "Sally, you're so creative. I'm just not."

I put down my latte without a sip. What about her remodel? Or the artistry in how she dressed? Perhaps she'd confused the word "creative" with "bohemian," a word that could better fit my style of windblown hair and minimally coordinated clothes. Or maybe she thought, like so many, that creativity was a rarified gift available only to a select few. In our star-studded, celebrity-obsessed culture, the word "creative" is often reserved for crazy-eyed inventors, high-tech gurus, fashion designers, or billionaires racing into space. "Jeannie, of course you're creative—everyone is! We just have our own expressions."

She smiled and then excused herself to go to the bathroom while I continued to mull this topic over.

Why don't we all see ourselves as creative? Why are the words "creative" or "creativity" applied only to things that are wildly original or "best in show"?

I say NO to this! Creativity is our birthright! Babies are born creative—cooing, crooning, and reaching out to experiment in their cribs. No toddler says, "I can't sing," unless someone has shut them down.

And, I get it. Getting shut down happens too often. A harsh word. A critique. Like what Mrs. Johnson, my third-grade chorus teacher said to me: "My dear, your voice is sticking out. Remember you are not a soloist." The humiliation still lives in my body. Tension creeps into my tongue the moment I open my mouth to sing in front of others. Then, not surprisingly, cracks and wobbles make it impossible for me to lead a round of "Happy Birthday."

Yet we all deserve to be able to sing! Why do we applaud The Three Tenors and stop inviting everyone to sing? Or pay thousands for paintings by recognized artists and not encourage all children to be artists as they play with paints? Or read best-selling blockbuster books but forget the power of writing in our journals?

We allow the critics and naysayers to kill the joy of creative play by saying things like, "What do you think this is?" and "You call this art?" and "You'll never be as good as . . ." Or, "Look out, you're going to screw this up."

Why do THEY get to decide what is art, what is creative, and what is beautiful? When did WE abnegate the right to choose what we love and find captivating? Why do we defer to the experts or the marketplace?

Creative expression is not a commodity to be measured!

As Jeannie returned with bright eyes and fresh lipstick, I was tempted to tell her that when she followed her passions, she was almost certainly being creative. But I decided to stay quiet until I had lived my quest a little longer. A good idea, because, as it turned out, I would need another decade before I really understood the power of creativity and play to feed our souls.

As Jeannie sat down, I admired my latte, reflecting on the barista's artistry to shape foam into a perfect heart.

The Eyes of Ikebana

*Why do we have to be sick or dying before we
can give ourselves permission to create?*
—SJF, AGE 55

*I*n the end, Japanese paper wrapping required more patience than I had, so I looked for new ways to express myself. I spent extra time designing my teaching handouts to make them more graphic and compelling. Sometimes, I took an extra minute to decorate the dining table or arrange food on a plate. And, occasionally, I cleaned my office to make it look calm and inviting, although my success in countering chaos in that space was short-lived.

In February 2006, my friend Ginger invited me to visit Cancer Lifeline, a Seattle-based nonprofit that she had recently been chosen to lead. Instead of tucking cancer into the dark shadows, this organization provides information and emotional support to patients, survivors, and their families as well as a safe space for them to talk about their experience with the disease. They also offer a variety of expressive arts and movement activities to aid in the recovery and coping processes.

As we toured the facility's two-story house, we passed a room of women silently writing. "Our journaling class," Ginger noted. Farther down the hall, one man and ten women made slow, bent-knee movements. "Tai Chi."

"I love this," I told her. "Everyone seems so engaged. It's a shame that so many of us wait until we have cancer to give ourselves time to create."

Why am I waiting? Isn't it time to stop procrastinating?

Walking up the stairs to the second floor, we passed a series of papier-mâché busts covered with paint, drawings, collage materials, and symbolism. Ginger smiled. "These women are honoring their new chests."

In an arts and crafts room, magazines lay piled against the walls waiting to be cut for collage work. A collection of Japanese vases sat near the sink, and I noticed a sign on the door that said "Ikebana class at 2 pm."

"Oh my God!" I exclaimed. "I don't have cancer, but I'd love to take an ikebana class. I love working with flowers." As a child in Connecticut, I enjoyed picking the daisies, foxgloves, roses, and rhododendrons that grew in our suburban garden and arranging them into bouquets for my mother. Later, as an adult, I filled vases with flowers I bought at grocery stores.

Ginger tilted her head. "Your dad had cancer; you could sign up today."

Ten minutes later, my name was on the roster.

At my first class session, the teacher, Nobuko-san, said, "In ikebana, we do not fill vase with flowers. We honor the life within flowers and natural materials. They are already beautiful, so with ikebana, we must make them more beautiful. We give them room to breathe. We want to see the space."

As the six class participants bent over their branches and flowers, pushing their materials gently into their *kenzan* (needlepoint holders), Nobuko-san continued her introduction for me, her one new student that day. "My school, Sogetsu school, is most modern ikebana. We give you textbook with principles. After you learn and train your eye to see, you can do many things your way."

She opened her textbook to the first lesson and placed camellia branches and chrysanthemum flowers in front of me. I stared at them while she continued. "Each lesson shows you right proportion for the material."

She picked up a camellia branch and gazed at it slowly before anchoring it in the kenzan that sat at the bottom of a flat, round dish with low sides. She continued placing the other materials, contemplating each item before positioning it according to the dimensions outlined in the textbook. Then, she cut the woody stems and bent them slowly into arching lines. "These give us the line while these flowers will give mass."

I looked at her hands, chiseled by age and four decades of teaching. Her fingers moved as if they always knew what to do. She used scissors to snip off a leaf here, a branch there. Then she stood back and considered her work. After viewing it from several directions, she removed three more leaves. It looked perfect.

Then, as I gasped, Nobuko-san took the whole thing apart and returned the materials to piles on the table. "Now you try!" she said.

I began by bending the camellia branch until I heard it snap. Nobuko-san quietly gave me another, and this time, I managed to bend it. I positioned it into the kenzan, after pricking my third finger.

"Very good," she said, when I had finished.

Nobuko-san's way of teaching captivated me. She offered suggestions yet always found something encouraging to say about each arrangement. In this judgment-free environment, class members cheered each other on.

Despite the meditative nature of ikebana, the participants were a rowdy bunch. Living with cancer and death seemed to have given them both a sense of humor and a perspective on what mattered. Here, I didn't have to take myself so seriously. I could giggle, groan, or occasionally swear when my arrangement keeled over just as I was inserting the last branch. Nobuko-san, who was born in Japan but was married to an American, welcomed the levity.

Ikebana slowed me down and invited me to feel the nature of my materials as I envisioned putting them into a container. Then, as I started, I tried to feel what was essential to my piece and pare away what was not. After I finished, I'd pause, clean up my space, and turn to Nobuko-san. "Nobuko-san, would you mind looking at my arrangement?"

She'd walk over, consider my work from several directions, and always find something appreciative to say. Nobuko-san encouraged my beginner attempts, reminding me that, although she had been teaching for decades, she was always learning. I would stand behind her to see my arrangement through her eyes. Then, after inspecting my piece, she'd invariably ask, "Do you mind?" before snipping off another branch, shifting the angle of a flower, or turning the container a few degrees. Her slight changes transformed my work and taught me to see what I missed. Over the next five years, whenever Cancer Lifeline offered a series of ikebana classes, I made sure to attend.

The class opened my eyes to new ways of seeing the natural world. Walking back to my car after two hours of ikebana, I viewed the world like an arrangement. Tall irises provided a sense of line in a neighborhood garden, while a cluster of rhododendron blooms suggested mass. The branches on a nearby madrona tree appeared to have been hand-twisted by a sculptor. I saw the negative spaces between trees and felt so grateful for the beauty that surrounded me.

I just had to choose to notice it.

Compare and Compete

*I*kebana class offered relief from the self-critical voice that had haunted me since childhood. In my family, self-judgment was like a curse passed down through the generations. My paternal grandmother, whom I loved for both her kindness to me and her gorgeous waist-length white hair, had been a stern mother to her fun-loving younger son. Dad grew up receiving regular doses of love laced with middle-America moralism, strict standards, and judgment. He admired his brilliant older brother, to whom he compared himself throughout his life. Even as middle-aged men, they'd hold intellectual jousts at our family dinners—debates I doubt my father ever won.

Critical of himself, Dad was also critical of his children. He wasn't deliberately cruel, but he had high standards for how things should be done. When one of us presented him with a drawing of a bird, Dad would judge it for its realism. He'd offer his analysis, effectively squeezing the delight out of sharing artwork with him.

From his college photo albums and sketches, I knew Dad had been an artist, a dimple-faced comedian, a skilled photographer, and a good sketcher. When he shipped off to the Gilbert Islands at the beginning of World War II, he made friends with the islanders and wrote stories about them. A series of wartime photos captured Dad bare-chested in a grass skirt, grinning as he attempted to dance the hula.

Throughout his three-and-a-half years at war, Dad corresponded almost daily with his wife. He filled stacks of thin airmail letters with

32

tales of life on the islands, his service experience, and his love for her. In the last of his wartime letters, his tone changed as he pleaded, "Has something changed between us? Why aren't you writing more?"

I didn't learn about Dad's first marriage until I was 13 and asked my mom an innocent question. I was helping her polish the silver—a massive task that took several hours. I dipped each fork into the gooey pink cream, rubbed the cleaner between the tines with my fingers to release the black tarnish, dipped the fork into water, and then dried it with a rag before it spotted. Rinse and repeat 16 times. After finishing one set of forks, I was about to start on the next when I asked, "Why do we have two sets of silver?"

"One set is from your dad's first marriage," she said matter-of-factly. "His wife gave back the silver engraved with Fs since she was no longer a Fox."

WHAAAATTT? My dad's first marriage? Why am I just finding out about this? He'd been with another woman? Instead of screaming, I took a deep breath and pummeled her with more questions, "Who was she? Did they have kids?"

"No, it was short. They married right before the war and got divorced when he came home."

"But who was she?" I wanted to be able to picture her.

My mother shrugged. "I think she was a journalist. She worked for *Time* magazine."

"Is she around?"

"No, she's dead now."

My mouth must have been hanging somewhere around my knees, despite the calm tone my mother continued to use. "How come you never told us?"

"There was no need. Your father doesn't talk about it."

I ran into our family room and pulled Dad's old scrapbooks out of the bookcase. I couldn't find *her*, but I saw places where four white photo corners surrounded an empty space. In the middle of one album, I found a beautiful sketch of a mystery woman. Mom confirmed it was *her*.

The stack of love letters to Dad's first wife lay hidden in the back of a closet for decades. Mom found them near the end of Dad's life, as my parents were preparing to move. My siblings and I decided that she didn't need to read them, seeing as she was already upset with Dad for dying. I took the letters home and scanned the last ones, along with the final letter from *her*. "I'm not who you think I am," she wrote. "I tried to be faithful because you're a good man, but it wasn't in me. I thought, in marrying you, I could change, but I was never meant to only be with one man. I've met another guy and have been living with him. I want a divorce." Reading this broke my heart.

As a young child, I intuitively sensed that Dad carried sadness, even though he could be social and witty at parties. I wanted to help heal him, although I didn't know how. So, I tried to earn his affection by trying to "do things right" and by imitating him. As a teenager, I debated him at the kitchen table, trying to match wits or convince him that the Vietnam War was wrong. Taking him on intellectually was a doomed strategy for getting what I really wanted: affection.

I never doubted that Dad loved me, but it took me decades to understand that he had offered me affection in all the ways he could.

At 50, Dad lost his job as a corporate planner and moved our family from Connecticut to New Jersey for a new position with a not-for-profit institution. Free of the stresses of trying to climb the corporate ladder, he returned to art and spent his weekends and evenings taking classes, reading books, and painting. Watercolors, sketching, oils, and block printing helped him reclaim a piece of himself. When I visited my parents' home on a vacation from graduate school at age 25, Dad's work hung on all the walls. Some of it hangs in my house today.

After his death, I found a faded copy of a flier for his first and only art exhibition. In it, he answered the question, "Why did you wait so long to study watercolors?" with "I never figured I was talented." *How could Dad not have seen himself as talented?* Then, I understood. He had carried the disease of self-criticism—the one I inherited.

My self-judgment and need to prove myself intensified when I was six. At that time, our family lived in an affluent Connecticut suburb. People jokingly referred to New Canaan as "the new land of milk and honey"—a mecca for New Yorkers wanting to flee the big city. New Canaan offered excellent schools, art exhibits, and musical performances, along with fresh air, trees, and the beauty of still-forested hills and Revolutionary-Era stone walls.

Despite its beauty and cultural advantages, New Canaan was a materialistically focused, competitive community. In our town, it wasn't enough to keep up with the proverbial Joneses; you had to outrun them. Comparing yourself to others was a sport played on an Olympic level. No matter how much money, talent, or recognition you gained, it was never enough.

We were a middle-class family in the land of the uber-rich. My schoolmates belonged to country clubs and rode at the prestigious New Canaan Mounted Police, where, as a horse-crazy girl, I longed to ride. They bought their outfits at a preppy local store called "The Villager." At 12, my best friend informed me that if I ever wanted to be popular, I would have to buy coordinated clothes. She suggested heading to The Villager and stocking up on matching ribboned cardigans, A-line skirts, oxford shirts, and knee socks. When I told my mother that my homemade clothes and hand-me-downs were thwarting my hopes for social success, she scowled and said, "Your father and I are saving for your college tuition." I shuffled off to the bedroom, feeling doomed.

In New Canaan, pressure to go to college started young. By my first day in second grade, I knew that attending Harvard or another Ivy League university was the key to a good life. The school divided our class into three learning levels: "A," "B," and "C." We all knew these stood for "fast, medium, and slow." At seven years old, I already understood that if I wanted a shot at Harvard, I had to remain in the "A" track to be able to take advanced placement classes nine years later in high school.

Fortunately, school came naturally to me. I could decipher a correct answer on a multiple-choice test and give my teachers back what they wanted. My rewards for being a good student were high grades, parental applause, and a secured seat in the fast track. But there were costs too. I could not fail, set my own standards for success, or veer away from a traditional path.

When it came time to go to college, I prioritized community over competition and chose to attend Oberlin College in Ohio. Over time, my solid academic skills helped me earn three graduate degrees—including a doctorate—and launch my career in education. Like many women wanting to succeed, I competed in environments that didn't honor my caring and creativity. I kept my wild, messy, and intuitive parts hidden, and I didn't talk about my spiritual interests. I sacrificed any freedom I might have had to make mistakes, appear foolish, or build castles that would wash away in the sand.

I was also never satisfied. For example, when I prepared my university or corporate courses, I tormented myself by imagining how others would have created more effective designs. Because what I did never felt like enough, I often pushed myself to read yet one more book right before class.

A writing teacher of mine, Ann Randolph, says, "Comparison kills creativity." By her logic, I slaughtered my creative impulse early on.

Fortunately, there were a few places in my childhood where the spirit of comparison didn't enter. One of them was in the woods.

Into the Woods

While the neighborhood girls played with Barbie dolls, I spent my afternoons as a young girl roaming the woods. After school, I'd swap my good-girl oxfords and knee socks for sweatshirts and sneakers and run to the back of our property. There, I'd push aside a curtain of inchworms dangling from the birches and scramble across the stone wall built by some farmer in the last century. I'd pick a deer path to follow and set off. Soon, I'd be in my sanctuary of stillness, where the silence was punctuated only by the rustling wind, the sounds of wood thrush, warblers, and woodpeckers, and the occasional darting of a squirrel or cottontail.

The wind called to me, and the glistening streambeds tempted me to follow them farther from home than I thought I should. The occasional arrowhead reminded me of how Menunkatuck and Saugatuck natives once roamed these same woods.

The forest carried different moods. In the birch grove, the air felt bright and welcoming; in the marsh, it felt dark and threatening. Occasionally, I'd be stopped by a dense thicket of brambles. When I realized I was lost, my heart would quicken, and I'd bushwhack until I reached a trail I knew.

For the most part, I felt connected to the spirit of the woods and was only rarely scared—like on the one day I broke the rules. I knew the large marsh full of skunk cabbage was off-limits. I'd heard that a child could get sucked into its treacherous mud. But I tested this anyway, in the dead of winter, when the swamp was frozen. After trying to determine the solidity of the ice with a few toe taps, I headed out to explore.

I'd only gone ten steps when I heard the ice crack and felt myself sink. Soon, my boots were lodged under the ice and freezing water began to fill them. I yanked and yanked but could only free one.

I'm in big trouble. I've lost a boot and my parents will know what I did.

I slid my foot out of the other and hobbled home with one stockinged foot. A worried mom welcomed me and warmed my toes, hoping to save them from frostbite damage. I don't remember receiving a lecture, but I never wandered into the swamp again. It remained the land of dark mystery.

In the evenings, I made up plots based on my adventures. On one expedition, I found the remains of a stone building, which I was sure must have been a Revolutionary-Era fort. In my tale, scrappy American soldiers stuck muskets out of the fort's small window slats, protecting the land from approaching British Redcoats.

When I reached junior high school, academics, clubs, and teen activities replaced my wandering. By the time we moved to New Jersey, I was 15 and had stopped going into the woods altogether. I didn't realize the extent to which they had been my sanctuary, a place to nourish my imagination free from any concern about others might think. I didn't realize how much I needed nature to fill my soul until years later, when I lived in cities like Paris, Washington, DC, and Manhattan. While I was drawn to their cultural life, I needed to spend big chunks of time in their parks.

I met my husband when he was living in the San Francisco area and I was in Seattle. But, it wasn't until we were married and living in Seattle that I realized he didn't share my love of cities. When I took him to visit my former neighborhood in Manhattan's Upper West Side, he looked at me in panic. "You liked this place?"

I had married a farm boy who grew up in Amherst, Massachusetts, a community where culture, education, and care for the land blended together. He liked Seattle, but he missed the opportunity to ride a tractor, run a chain saw, and care for a piece of property. As a result, when he retired, we began talking about how we might live in a more rural setting and still have access to Seattle's cultural life and our family and friends in the city.

At the time, I owned a horse—my childhood dream come true—and boarded him at a stable north of the city. Then, I moved him to Vashon Island (off the coast of Seattle) to work with the horse trainer with whom I had started riding at age 42. Three or four days a week, I'd commute to the island for our lessons. In the process, Vashon became a kind of second home. Seeing the lineup of cars waiting to leave the island on the morning ferries, though, I doubted I wanted a boat-dependent existence. Still, Steve and I grew curious about living there and approached a real estate agent "just to see" what kind of homes might be available. We weren't impressed by the first three we saw.

Good thing, because I'm not ready to leave Seattle.

Then, at the end of the 2006 holiday season, on a dreary cold day during which I wanted nothing more than to sit on the sofa with my tea and read, our agent, Emma, called. "If you want to live anywhere near where Sally keeps her horse, this is your property. But it goes on the market in two days and won't last. You need to come out today if you want a crack at it."

No thanks. Most of our property-viewing trips don't amount to anything, and this is a day for staying warm inside.

Steve challenged me, saying, "You know that we really trust Emma. If she says this might be it, we should go. Just think about what it would be like to live near the horse–or even keep him on the property. She says there won't be another like this."

Two hours later, we were on the island, in rain gear and muck boots.

"I don't know," I told Steve when he asked for my impressions. "It's a nice enough house. Nothing spectacular, though." But, before leaving, we decided to walk the five-acre property. Toward the back, four Douglas fir trees stood sentry, marking an entrance into the woods. We descended the path they guarded, crossing over a carpet of wild cyclamen edged with native salal. Majestic madrona trees with twisted copper branches glistened in the rain. The snowberries were blooming with tiny popcorn-like white balls at their tips. We walked underneath a natural archway formed by hazelnut branches that seemed to welcome us to this land of loamy soil and mystery. I breathed in the sweet smell of damp, rotting wood and heard the Goddess Diana, the huntress, singing.

As we reached the trail's end and returned to the house, a Muse-like voice whispered to me:

"Notice the magic you are feeling. Sense how the trees want to speak to you. Imagine what it would be like to be close to nature and wake up to birds, squirrels, raccoons, and deer. The calm will help you create, and the space speaks to you. This land could be a sanctuary for your transformation."

As Steve and I left the woods and walked back to the house, we watched a two-pronged buck and a doe grazing in the yard. They lifted their heads, noted our presence, and continued chomping on grass. I looked at Steve. "Honey," I said, "I love this."

Although the Muse had spoken, Steve and I tore our guts out trying to decide what to do. We talked about the house for two days. I thought, journaled and talked to friends. I prayed. Were we ready to leave our known world, our community, and move farther from my family?

I'm not ready. I'm not ready. Give me time.

We heard that another couple was preparing an offer to buy. Still, we couldn't decide.

On the third morning after seeing the house, Steve woke up and said, "I think we should do this."

I gulped as I thought about the losses we would face. But then I thought about the quiet, the smell of loam, the nearness to nature, and the words of the Muse. "OK. Let's do it," I said.

We made an offer that morning. It was accepted the next day.

Becoming a Gardener

The move to the island changed our lives. The ferry became more of an obstacle to off-island adventures than anticipated, so we immersed ourselves in our new community, enjoying the benefits of a small town—like knowing we'd always run into someone we knew at the supermarket.

Much to my surprise, at the age of 56, I turned into a gardener. I had always HATED gardening growing up. In my childhood suburban neighborhood, gardening meant sticking foundation shrubs around houses, adding a few ground covers, and popping in a few petunias and geraniums for decoration in the summer. Knowing weeds always return, I wondered why anyone would indenture themselves to this Sisyphean activity. Flowers could be bought in stores.

But on the island, I was fueled by memories of Japan. And, it seemed like someone must have injected a desire to garden into the island water. I felt driven to dig. Like many new converts, though, I was cursed with over-zealotry. Experienced and knowledgeable gardening friends urged me to take it slow. "Give yourself a year before you do any major work," they said.

A year? Way too long. I'm 56, and I want to see my new copper beech sapling become a tree. I want to harvest blueberries and apples from an orchard. I can't afford to wait.

My next creative project had fallen into my lap. At night, I read books and magazines about gardens; by day, I created. At the end of our first summer, Steve and I ripped out an unimpressive chokecherry tree next to our back patio to allow space for a flower bed—a home for my first peonies. I wanted things to be just right for the six tubers I had bought: two each of white, pink, and magenta. I spent hours on the computer reading about how to plant, fertilize, and care for them. I inspected each root looking for its tumescent eyes—the signs of new life that would need to be placed face-up in the soil. I dug a long, two-foot-deep trench to break up the dense earth, then refilled it and inserted the tubers, leaving plenty of room between them and no more than two inches of dirt on top. I completed the bed with a variety of flowers—roses, salvia, penstemon, and lavender—to keep the peonies company while they slept through their first winter.

Some inner gardening valve was stuck on "on," so I kept digging. We had salvaged a lone pink dogwood that the buyers of our Seattle house didn't want, so I designed a curved bed to house and honor her. Soon after, we built a small pond nearby.

Over the next three years, I designed a shade garden, installed a 1,200-square-foot vegetable plot (was I planning to feed an army?), and planted an orchard with 15 apple, plum, cherry, and pear seedlings. I tore out invasive plants in the woods and created two ginormous woodland gardens. I took classes and completed a Master Gardener program as part of my "DIY horticulture degree." I read everything I could about gardening in the Northwest. In my second year of gardening mania, the local garden club invited me to be their president, based, I'm sure, on my exuberance. Gardening felt fresh and vibrant, unlike the leadership classes I still directed in Seattle, which had started to feel stale. My teaching vocabulary changed as I introduced words like "cultivate," "germinate," "harvest," and "fallow" in speaking about an organization's life.

Our land filled me with enough energy to work long hours in the garden—energy which I wish I still had now! One afternoon, as I peeled back vines and brambles in a shaded area, I discovered a pile of broken glass, bottles, twisted metal, and car parts. It turns out that part of our property had been used as the neighborhood's unauthorized dump zone. As I cleared out debris, I almost heard the garden sigh in relief. I started to feel like I was truly in relationship with this land.

Swept into the spirit of partnership, I felt the section of garden talking to me. An old tree stump surfaced and became a ten-foot sculpture in the midst of this once unloved area. I stood awed by the way it captured the golden late-afternoon light. Then, a flood of messages poured in: "Plant sword ferns here," "Add rhododendrons," and "Frame the area with liriope," a low-growing, grass-like, variegated plant. It was as if a Muse had appeared, imbuing the area with magic. I worked furiously, using every bit of remaining light left in the day. As night took over, my communion ended, and I returned to the house.

The next day, when I returned to the garden, the Muse had gone. But my memory of connecting intuitively with the land stayed with me. And, the feeling would surface again, from time to time, over the next five years—along with the sense of being guided in my search for more meaning, beauty, and connection. I didn't know who or what was guiding me, but it almost didn't matter. I was being led by the joy of discovery and creation. By the following spring, when my peonies sprung forth into their first beautiful blossoms, new parts of me were beginning to bloom as well.

Aging, Improvised

How Much Time Do I Have?

I've heard it said that real gardeners plant trees they will never see mature. I knew it would take years before my 20 newly planted birches, pines, spruces, maples, and copper beech would reach even half their eventual height. That reality prompted some serious questions: *Would I see that? How long would Steve and I be on our island property? And how much time did we have left together?*

When we were first married, I barely thought about the 16-year age spread between us, trusting that his young spirit would carry the day. But, by the time Steve was 70, I wasn't so sanguine. One afternoon, we were enjoying coffee and croissants at our favorite island café when he said, "I don't think you accept the fact that I'm turning 70."

My appetite instantly disappeared.

"You're right. I don't." Age had never been an issue for us, but that was changing. For his first 70 years, Steve had few medical issues and rarely needed medications. Then, at his yearly physical, his doctor announced, "Your heart is racing erratically. You can see it on this EKG. We need to calm the fibrillation before it damages the heart. Would you like me to perform the procedure here, or would you prefer to go to the hospital?"

The next day, Steve entered the hospital for the first of many surgeries that would take place over the next ten years.

Steve is my anchor; everyone with creative aspirations should be so lucky as to have a partner like him. I call him "my ground" or "my rock," and his presence has always been so steady and count-on-able that any change to his health or stamina felt like a seismic shift to me.

When we met, he was intelligent, caring, funny, appreciative, and sexy. That's all still true, although sexy at age 86 looks different from the way it did at age 52. Older sexy doesn't depend on strong abs, bulging arm muscles, great stamina, or a ready libido. It lives in intimate conversations, trust, holding hands, eating popcorn, and playing with the dogs. When I worry about how long we will have together, sexy looks like still being alive.

Although Steve once called me "high maintenance"—which meant, I think, that all of my interests have asked a lot of our household—he loves me very much. To this day, I continue to bring learnings, classes, work, spiritual pursuits, and animals into our lives. My role in our household is "chief explorer and stirrer-upper," while Steve keeps watch over our cars, ensures our home and property function, and anchors everything I do. He's also the most grateful person I've ever met.

Writing our wills was difficult. I am a rational being, and I knew about their importance. But Steve and I delayed preparing anything more than notarized DIY versions for 25 years. We "never had time" as we did the really important stuff like take vacations, care for the animals, read books, meditate, or clip our toenails—i.e., almost anything else.

On the eve of Steve's hip surgery, we crossed the line and decided to see a lawyer. Steve was 86 at that point, and friends kept telling us about older people they knew who hadn't returned from their hip surgeries—not exactly what I wanted to hear on the eve of Steve's. We hired a Seattle lawyer who, thankfully, was willing to meet with us in his Vashon farmhouse. I thought dealing with our modest estate would be a no-brainer, but still, there were questions to think about. Steve had two sons, both in their fifties with families. I had never had children. How would we honor his children and still give to the charities that were important to me? And would the "estate plan" our lawyer was suggesting—a big term for a small holding—limit my freedom after Steve died and our money was split in two parts? My stomach clenched as the lawyer discussed options, and worry nibbled on the walls of my gut. Who would be there for me after Steve died if our health-related needs drained our resources? I loved his sons and their families; yet I felt uneasy.

They are not my biological children. They have no obligation to help me when Steve is gone.

The smart me could say, *"No child has an obligation to any parent. Besides, you all love each other."* The scared me, though, said, *"You're going to be alone."*

I didn't share such thoughts with our lawyer, and I eventually relaxed as he explained the merits of preparing a will. What we came up with almost didn't mean as much to me as the fact that we came up with something. We had crossed a threshold and were willing to look at an inevitable part of our future.

Signs of Age

As I moved through my fifties, age didn't faze me because I didn't feel old. When my doctors complimented me on how well I was doing (subtext: "given your age . . .") I fantasized about turning and saying, "Thanks, junior."

However, as I moved into my late fifties, my body let me know that changes were underway. The once beautiful flesh on my high cheekbones—one of my few beauty assets—began a slow death march toward my jowls. The gap between my front teeth kept growing, and I began photoshopping the portraits on my new website, so my mouth didn't look like I had a piece of dark spinach stuck in it.

At my yearly doctor's exam, a medical assistant with tattooed arms and purple scrubs instructed me to stand on the scales. She moved a metal bar over my head and announced, "5'4"."

"There must be a mistake," I countered. "I've always been 5'5 1/2"."

"You look at the scale," she said, more interested in moving me into the exam room than debating the results. I glanced at the marker: Yep, it said 5'4". Apparently, nearly two inches of me had gone rogue. Where were they? I had NOT given my body permission to shrink.

Was my body betraying me?

The culprit might have been my bones. I couldn't have spelled "osteoporosis" in my fifties, let alone define it. Then, the results of my first DEXA bone density scan at age 65 produced unexpected bad news: I had a severe case of it. "Your numbers aren't good," my doctor said. "Your bones aren't dense enough, and a fall could lead to a break." She let me know this was the kiss of near-death for any older person. "I want you on medication right away." (I had always thought doctors were supposed to put things positively.) The idea of better living through chemicals didn't thrill me, especially since my doctor didn't promise the return of my missing inches.

What else might I lose in the night if I didn't stand guard against the approaching forces of aging? To create, I needed a well-functioning body—whether to shovel dirt, clip flowers, use my vocal cords, or type on a keyboard. My body was my companion on my journey, even if I hadn't given it all the respect and care it deserved over the years. I was happy about what it still could do, but my list of limitations kept growing. I could no longer:

~ Pick up heavy objects

~ Walk, dance, sit, or garden for long periods without aching

~ Have enough time or energy for everything I wanted to do

I had always taught my students that they could use "design thinking" to turn constraints into opportunities. I, however, didn't like the limits I was facing, and doses of pain didn't do anything for my creative juice. And yet, aging was clearly happening, regardless of my feelings about it. I knew I was going to need some tools to help me through what felt like more a concrete barricade than a "constraint."

So, I invented a mantra to help me with aging:

In the face of what I am losing, I am grateful for what I still have.

And that got me started on what I really needed—a new narrative with which to approach the years ahead.

Retiring Retirement

As I neared 60, my need for a hopeful-yet-realistic story about aging intensified. The obvious narrative revolved around "retirement," the only word I'd ever heard used in the context of aging when I was young. That term, which, to me, meant stopping, disengaging, or moving away from something, sounded dismal.

When people asked, "Are you retired?" on questionnaires or at parties, I'd flash them my best deer-in-the-headlights look while figuring out what to say. Had I cut back on paid work? Yes. Was I still making money—society's metric for a successful American life? Some, but not nearly what I had made before. Writing, a mostly unpaid endeavor, was consuming much of my energy. "Not exactly," I'd say, and then stumble through some cobbled-together description of what I was doing with my time.

Retirement suggested something dusty—the kind of thing you might store on a shelf in a museum. Not only did it not fit me, but it also didn't fit my friends working hard as artists or as caretakers for their parents or grandchildren. It didn't include colleagues about to start businesses or acquaintances squeezed out of the workforce who wanted to get back in. We were all engaged and working, regardless of whether or not we were making money.

"Are you retired?" was a binary (yes/no) question that applied best to people who might someday receive a going-away party or a gold watch. The United States' social security system, the safety net that had allowed many people older than I to retire, was designed for folks like my grandfather. He was born in the 1890s, went to work for Bell Telephone in 1910, and was set loose with a pension and social security when he was 65.

I find it interesting that the designers of our social security system borrowed freely from the German pension system created in the 1880s by the aristocratic and manipulative politician, Otto von Bismarck. That crafty dude tried to keep government workers out of the clutches of socialism by offering them pensions if they made it to age 70 (few did). When the government booted him out, they reset the pension-eligible age to 65. We here in the U.S. borrowed that number and established it as our retirement age as well. After social security was launched, age 65 became synonymous with "freedom from work" and "getting old." If you were crazy enough to want to work beyond it, the system penalized you—at least until rules changed in the 1990s.

My grandfather made retirement living look good. I knew him as a kind, white-haired man who spent his days braiding rugs, pickling watermelon with my grandmother, and puttering in his basement work-shop. Every week, he put on a tweed jacket and went downtown to visit with his men friends at the Wednesday meeting of "The Dun Working Club." I adored my grandfather and loved it when he read to me from his overstuffed leather chair. I'd crawl into his lap and beg to see the gold watch he carried in his pocket. He'd reach behind his suspenders, dig into his baggy wool pants, and pull it out on its golden chain. As he twirled it for me in the sun, he'd say, "The Company gave it to me."

My father might have expected a gold watch and similar retirement, but by the 1980s, when Dad retired, the world had changed. Women's rights, civil rights, Vietnam, and sociopolitical upheavals had rocked the boat. My mother, who spent her twenties, thirties, and early forties as a traditional homemaker, returned to work, teaching pre-school in her mid-forties. She went back to school, earned a master's degree at age

52, and had no intention of stopping work just because my father, ten years her senior, wanted to retire. Better that he learned to cook dinner, which he did, as his role shifted to helping at home, volunteering, and making art.

My parents' life together never fit the image of the happy, stress-free retirement I saw portrayed in magazine ads. In them, a handsome white-haired couple sat on the deck of their lakefront estate, clinking glasses of red wine and celebrating success. The photos promoted a fantasy. For starters, few of us would ever enjoy their affluence. And, if that couple was anything like the people I knew, they would discover the following day that their deck had rotted and needed massive repairs. Or, they would receive a call from the doctor confirming that the wife's stomach problems were the result of pancreatic cancer. They might learn that their daughter was in jail on drug charges and their belligerent 16-year-old granddaughter would be coming to live with them. Whoever created the marketing phrases "the golden years" or "leisure living" obviously hadn't experienced these uncertainties, losses, or difficulties.

So, I kept looking for aging stories.

One of the ones I found, the "you don't have to die" narrative, did not seem worthy of consideration, at least to anyone mindful of natural laws.

Then, there was the "super-elder" story—the one that included colorful videos of an 80-year-old gymnast still doing splits. Given that I had never been able to do a split, her success seemed irrelevant. And my former athleticism wasn't likely to return. Touting the elders who lived at the far edges of what was physically possible didn't help the rest of us.

These saccharine stories tried to offer hope but failed, the way artificial sweeteners can never replace the goodness of honey.

I wanted a realistic narrative—one that promoted engagement rather than retirement. Researcher Mihaly Csikszentmihalyi discovered that when people work on a project that fully engages them, they can enter an elevated state of timeless absorption he calls "flow." I experienced flow when I spoke in public and felt thoroughly connected to my audience, when I wrote a poem and felt the words were speaking themselves through me, or when I dug in my garden.

The story I was shaping for myself was built around engagement—and expressing myself creatively was my path into flow.

Improvising

As it became clearer and clearer to me that creativity was the guiding light that would help me navigate aging, I continued to experiment with just about any art form that struck my fancy.

I thought that, at 58, I might be too old for improvisational theater. But my few experiences with "improv" were so much fun I decided to sign up for a class anyway. As I ferried to Seattle for the first session, I wondered what mix of young comedians and Robin Williams wannabes I would find. Would everyone be trying to out-clever each other like the contestants in the competitive improv I had seen on TV?

I was relieved to see a diverse mix of faces when I walked into the dusty, black-walled theater space. In addition to differences in races and gender, there was enough gray hair in the room to make me feel at home.

Laughter is a great unifier, and the instructor, Matt Smith, a well-known Seattle improviser, had us in stitches within moments of starting class. From his rambling monologue, I calculated his age to be close to mine—a comforting bonus.

Improv is a participant sport, so, as soon as Matt finished his stories, he launched a game that had us offering each other crazy noises and gestures. Then, he introduced the "failure bow," an official permission to fall, screw up, and have fun, no matter what. "When you fail," he said, "I want you to celebrate. Throw your arms up into the air with a dumb-ass grin, and yell, 'Thank you, I failed!'"

In my youth, botching something in public was reason to freeze or disappear into the ether—NOT take a bow. My instincts to get things right were so highly tooled that I could barely imagine another outlook on life. I totally got it when Matt spoke about operating in "cringe mode," a state of anticipatory shame in which we feel humiliation before we even make a mistake.

In class, action—rather than psychoanalysis—was the cure for cringing. I soon was throwing my arms into the air along with others and laughing. "I failed! I failed!" I shouted repeatedly.

After mastering celebratory failure, we practiced the classic improv exercise "Yes, and" in pairs. Our job was to keep a volley of dialogue going by responding positively to whatever our partners said before we offered back our comments. Playing "Yes, and" didn't require being quick or clever; it just required a willingness to be present to our partners, listen, and react—a good thing, since being quick and clever was not my forte. I was smart; or, at least, "the smart one" was the role given to me in my family. (I would have preferred "the cute and pretty one," but that role was taken.) Being seen as intelligent helped me in school, although it came with a price. When you're supposed to be bright, you can't let anyone see how lost or confused you feel. And you can't risk looking stupid. I only responded to classroom questions when I knew I had the correct answer. Improv class challenged that behavior pattern. I had to enter a scene or step on stage *before* I had an answer or knew what I was doing.

For example, Matt had two people stand in front of our group and invent a sketch based on the theme "in the laundromat." The players were to continue until someone new entered and tapped one of them to leave. My mind spun as I watched the first performers and started plotting.

I'd better start thinking up something to say now so I can go in and look good.

Matt yelled, "Don't think it out in advance. Just commit and go. You'll discover what to do once you're out there." I sat still with my mental engines revving, looking for the right moment to join. Finally, something shifted. I jumped in, tapped a player, and said something. I have no recollection of what it was, but I know I heard laughter. Magic! With that, I relaxed. When I got tagged to leave, I couldn't wait to get back in.

The spirit of play infected me, and I discovered that my imagination was more than ready to offer plenty of ideas and images once I let go of trying to "be good." Goofier parts of me came out over the course of the eight sessions with Matt.

I particularly loved character work because it allowed me to put my natural empathy and interest in people to use. When I played an elderly woman crossing the street, I wanted to know how she viewed her world. I tried to enter her body, see through her eyes, breathe like she would breathe, and walk as she walked. I found that my body naturally bent over, and my hand started shaking. Fast-approaching cars felt threatening, and their noise was overwhelming. I was literally experiencing someone else's world.

Being in character for just ten minutes shifted how I saw the residents at my mother's assisted care unit. When I had first wheeled Mom into the dining room of her facility, I was dismayed by what I saw—an assortment of wheelchairs, walkers, oxygen tanks, and heads leaning toward their plates. The residents looked to me like a faceless group. After I played that old woman, however, they became people. As I sat at my mom's table with them, I imagined being in their bodies. I wondered who they had been in their youths, what felt risky to them, and what made them happy. I asked them these questions when I could. And I felt the loss when one of them died.

As I continued my journey with aging, I became increasingly aware of—and appalled by—how our culture disrespects older people. What was most disturbing to me was that I had shared this attitude for years. Ageism is a mindset that dismisses and diminishes the people we will someday become. It robs us of some of the life ahead of us.

I remember walking into my first meeting of the Vashon Island Garden Club, shortly after Steve and I moved to the island. As I stepped into the local church parish hall as a 56-year-old, I thought, "Jeez, there's a lot of gray hair here. What do I have in common with these people?" The joke was that I was already dying my gray hair!

Once I got to know the members and learned their stories, I found them to be amazing individuals. They had been mothers, lawyers, caretakers, entrepreneurs, civic heads, doctors, and more. Their volunteer contributions to local organizations—including the food bank, the arts center, the animal welfare organization, the land trust, and a variety of youth programs—kept our community afloat. Over time, they became my role models for healthy, engaged aging. But, on that first day with the group, I couldn't see any of that through my "too old" and "gray hair" filters.

When aging appeared on the faces of people I loved, I didn't need to avoid it. So, I began seeing older people through the lens of those I cared about. Eighty-two years old looked like Steve. Ninety-two looked like my Mom. Then, when I experienced aging by embodying it through a character or imaginative possibility, it became less forbidding.

If we all brought improv to aging, would it help us see more possibilities? Could walking in another's shoes—if only for a moment—help lift the weight of ageism?

If I wanted to live a new story about aging, I needed to be vigilant about all the ways ageism still influenced me.

Digging for a Purpose

Another way I could release the compulsion of "having to be good" or "getting things right" was by using my body to play. When I was in improv class, lying on my back and squiggling like a sloth hanging from a tree, I didn't worry about what I was doing. Moving helped release the grip of the mind.

And, as much as my mind sometimes squashed my freedom to experiment, I still appreciated the gifts it had given me. Some meditation teachers spoke about the mind like an enemy, a low-class citizen to be dismissed or avoided. Yet, mine had enabled me to earn three graduate degrees, solve innumerable work and life problems, and succeed in a meaningful career. I didn't want to lose my mind; I wanted to integrate it with my intuition and body awareness. I needed my mind, feelings, and body working together to answer the big question I pondered, *What purpose do I see for myself in the years ahead?*

Research suggested that having a sense of purpose was key to a long, healthy life, and that, from my experience, felt right. At the same time, something about the words "having a purpose" made me cringe. It felt so cognitive and hackneyed. Perhaps I was rebelling against the growing "purpose industry" of books and seminars. When I searched on Amazon for "finding your purpose," over 7,000 entries jumped out. I would read one of the purpose books occasionally, looking for an idea that could help my path, but I rarely found what I needed.

In my thirties, I sought a sense of purpose and direction for my career by attending transformational seminars. I sat for hours in straight-backed hotel room chairs, trying to noodle myself into some form of comfort without banging into the participant next to me, whose chair was fastened to mine. Motivational speakers cheered our "breakthrough" insights while I had visions of the upcoming bathroom break. I willed my body to tough it out while a Hollywood-style trainer boomed, "Turn to your neighbor and tell them what new possibility is opening up for you." Fortunately, I could always invent something. On the last day of a particularly pressure-cooked seminar, I stood and announced the meaning of my life to a chorus of rousing applause. I have no idea what I said.

As I approached my big 6–0 birthday, I wanted whatever purpose was guiding me to feel right in my body and consistent with my Longing. Although I couldn't always translate a felt sense of rightness into words, I'd occasionally receive information from a Muse-like voice. One day, as I was planting dahlias, I heard, *"Dig as if your life depends on it."*

I decided to dig for my purpose, transforming my long hours in the garden into a kind of prayer. The fact that I didn't know what I was doing meant that I frequently moved plants around—offering more opportunities to dig. My obsessive digging produced a garden mainte-nance monster I would later regret, but I couldn't stop.

In the evenings, I wrote. I wrote about the crazy excursions Steve and I made to Seattle to dig up the plants we adopted. I wrote about the personalities of my trees and how my sense of self was changing as I fell increasingly in love with nature. I wrote about what it was like to be a beginner who was prone to many mistakes but kept on gardening anyway. Soon, I had a whole collection of writings, which I later shared with the 1,000 guests who visited our gardens as part of the Vashon Island Garden Tour.

With hindsight, I can see my purpose and direction was emerging with each shovelful of dirt, piece of writing, and improv class sketch.

But my clarity was obscured by thinking a purpose should be "mighty," and what I was doing didn't meet my high standards for worthiness. My gremlins took advantage of my doubts, jumping in and questioning the time I was devoting to writing and gardening. *"Too selfish,"* they said. *"Not significant enough when the world is in such terrible shape. You're spending so much time writing, and you're not even a writer."* Or, *"All this time in the garden is a distraction."*

I hoped that a voice from on high might send down a direction. Maybe I'd seen too many movies about a prophet standing on the mountaintop receiving the Holy Word. I had received a couple of significant messages over the years, and one of them changed the course of my career when I was working for the university. It announced, *"Design the Graduate Management Program NOW"*—a compelling directive that launched one of the most fruitful periods of my work life. Knowing I'd received what felt like a mandate gave me the courage to persevere with creating the program, even when doing so proved daunting.

Because of that experience, I had hoped to be blessed with a similar proclamation as I entered the next stage of my work. But, in my late fifties, it seemed that I had to discover my path by walking it and watching my footsteps instead of sighting on a distant goal. Each creative activity increased my awareness and led me to the next step. Ikebana taught me to appreciate space and the beauty of natural materials and the garden. Gardening invited me to notice nature and write about my experiences. Improv pushed me to play and step away from my getting-it-rightness.

In my late fifties, I was still coaching clients to help them find their own professional and personal directions. I might have told someone facing my dilemma, "Follow the trail of what you love, and let the rest emerge. Let that be purpose enough as you keep going. Find joy in what you do, and you'll find your way. Give yourself time and honor the unknown."

If only I could have trusted my own words!

But without my own coach, I found periods of liminality and transition to be challenging. It would be a few more years before I met a guide who could help me—in the form of an imaginal presence, a Muse I called "Isabel."

Before Isabel entered my life and became both my advisor and comforter, I relied on Steve. When the doubts felt overpowering, I'd find him in his office and beg for "couch time." He knew this was an SOS—code for "Please help me NOW." We'd go together to the sofa, where I'd snuggle in his arms and tell him about the waves of doubts, many of which he had heard. "I don't know what my purpose is," was a common opener.

Steve listened.

"What I'm doing doesn't feel like enough."

More listening. He'd then gently ask, "What would you like from me?"

"I don't know, but . . ."

"I think you need a hug." (He was always right on that.)

After a giant bear hug, he would continue. "What would you say to one of your clients?" The guy was (and is) brilliant.

"I'd tell them, 'You're fine. Nothing's wrong. You're doing the work. And maybe it's time to head back to the garden.'"

Gradually, I started to listen.

Performing

When I dug, I could reflect on where I was going or a problem I was trying to work through. I often thought about the polarities in my life, contradictory forces that are interdependent and permanently connected, using the "both/and" perspective I had learned from Barry Johnson, author of *Polarity Management*. As Barry told those of us who met regularly as part of a learning community, life was rarely "either/or."

Shovel in hand, I thought I about the polarities in my life:

Thrust shovel into the ground: "I have had many disappointments, *and* I am successful."

Throw dirt to the right: "I am a woman of faith, *and* I have many doubts."

Dig deeper into the hole: "I enjoy creating alone, *and* I need the love and support of friends."

Throw dirt: "I carry joy *and* sorrow."

As I dug, I also thought about what I wanted to share at a presentation I was scheduled to give at a gathering of our polarity thinking community in Chicago. I knew that the 40 members attending were used to staring at slides as they listened to their colleagues' scripted presentations. I wanted to do something different. I wanted to perform rather than present—ditching the PowerPoint in favor of speaking from the heart about the contradictions in my life and spiritual practices.

I wasn't sure how the group would respond to my openness and vulnerability. Yet this work was more than academic to me; it was personally relevant.

As I thought about aging, I was aware of the following polarities:

~ Age took away some of my capabilities *and* gave me new freedoms.

~ With age, I was nearer to death *and* could appreciate life more.

~ Age opened the door to creating *and* closed the door on what I would never be able to do.

My list of personal polarities kept expanding until it was time to select a few and sketch out what I would do. Inspired by Robin Williams—my hero with his generous spirit and wild, on-the-spot comedy that seemed to come from the ether—I wanted to improvise some of my talk. But, since I was no Robin, I also wanted to have notes hidden near me, just in case my brain went blank.

I arrived at the conference having told only one friend what I planned to do. I quaked as my 4 pm slot on the schedule—the last of the day—approached. At my allotted time, I surveyed the room, noticing how the posters from earlier sessions drooped on the walls. Even the sweaty water glasses atop the used white tablecloths looked pooped. People seemed weary from sitting all day.

As my colleagues returned from a break to listen to me, I surprised them. "Would you slide all these tables to the side so we could sit in rows, theater-style? I need room to move in front of you." A few people shot me odd looks, but most quickly obliged, happy for some quick exercise.

Then, heart pounding and head swirling, I stood in front of them and began walking back and forth across my small "stage," standing in the four quadrants of a "polarity map" I had taped off on the floor.

I moved to the far left and talked about needing to embrace tough reality. I moved to the far right and talked about the importance of hope. I moved to the near left quadrant and described the downside of tough reality devoid of hope—cynicism. I moved to the near right and addressed the shadow of hope without reality—wishful thinking and blind optimism. The physicality in my presentation relaxed me. And as I became surer of myself, my words flowed. I never needed my notes.

My job was to stay open, feel my audience, and trust that Spirit was guiding me during 35 minutes in front of the group. All my digging had helped me prepare. Now, my job was to let go and speak from a vulnerable-yet-wise part of myself. No need to worry about how I was doing or what others were thinking; I was in the zone, my flow state.

After I closed my talk, it felt hard to come back to the room. I stood vibrating, as silence filled the space. I knew people had been moved. Applause seemed superfluous, although it felt great when it finally came.

Later, some colleagues told me how courageous I had been to talk about my vulnerabilities and how much my doing so had meant to them. I thanked them but wanted to say,

It doesn't take courage when you feel like you're being guided. Feeling connected takes away the fear. What's scary is feeling confused and alone.

Later that evening, my friend Jake approached me with one of his big grins. "That was theatrical. You have to do more! What comes next?" I valued his opinions and loved this question. I had felt so alive performing, and I knew I was finding part of the answer I had been searching for as a Muse-like voice whispered:

This is you.

I didn't need to have a purpose I could articulate—I now had one I could live. In performing my story, I felt like I had discovered fire.

"It's Because You Are 60"

"It's Because You Are 60"

My sixties were my take-off, not my landing.
I had time!
-SJF, AGE 60

As my 60th birthday approached, I wondered how to celebrate it. Turning 50 had seemed easy, but 60 felt different; it was too big to ignore. From what I'd learned as a kid, 60 was *old*. I thought about hosting a party but nixed that idea. Neither my husband nor I were party-giving animals, and throwing one sounded exhausting. So, I invented a unique gift instead. I listed 60 experiences or low-cost luxuries I wanted to give myself over the coming year. My list included coffee with special friends, a laughter yoga class, a few long walks in favorite places, a trip to a local museum, and a clowning class. I added one particularly unconventional item—a face reading with Jean Haner.

I'd been intrigued with Jean's work for a couple of years. I'd always wondered why I'd been born with a small nose, given the humiliation it caused me growing up. Was there a meaning to my upturned nose? Or was my unusual appearance just a cross I had to bear? When I made the appointment with Jean, she asked me to send her portrait photos of me with my hair pulled back. As I attached them to an email, I cringed, thinking I couldn't look any uglier.

The morning of our telephone consultation, I waited nervously in the old blue recliner where I did my writing. But the moment I heard Jean's soft, melodic voice on the phone, I relaxed. She began to describe what different facial features signified in the traditional Chinese system that guided her work. The mouth, she said, is about fulfillment, and she saw in my mouth no signs of my not being fulfilled. She didn't take time to explain all the details behind this assessment, but no matter; I was pleased.

She said my chin suggested I would break from the past and move into a more empowered "yang" decade of my life. The markings on my chin indicated my tenacity and level of will, but they also suggested that I was depleted and might need more deep rest. My chin further indicated a love of taking action—which meant that I was at risk of running out of gas. That made sense to me.

She went on to say that people with smaller, shorter noses like mine work often work more efficiently and stay organized. (I thought about challenging that idea by showing her my desk.) Visible nostrils suggest someone who is generous with her energy and puts a lot into what she does—another reason to rest more. Everything she said rang true. And I didn't feel judged!

Jean explained that in the traditional Chinese system, challenges always accompany strengths. To her, my features revealed three areas I might want to address. In her words:

"You may overthink things and end up doubting yourself and feeling uncertain." (Check that!)

"You judge yourself harshly." (Double yup!)

"You are a gentle guide with many gifts to give." (Sounds good!)

When she asked about my career and plans, I effervesced as I described my new creative direction. I talked about wanting to tell stories, perform, and write. "Yes, yes, yes!" she said. "Everything you describe is a great fit."

I gushed on. "Jean, I don't want to retire. I'm finally figuring out what I'm meant to do, and I'm relaunching my consulting practice. I feel like this is my time."

Her enthusiasm rang through the phone line. "That sounds so right for you."

Although she was only confirming what I knew, her words sounded like a benediction.

I was about to do a happy dance when a fleet of gremlins charged the cabin, upset with the joy they saw me experiencing. They battered down my excitement with a set of assault statements: *"It's too late. You're too old to develop as a writer or performer. You should have started years ago."*

After listening to them, my voice dropped. "Jean, if I was meant to do all this, I should have started 40 years ago. My friends are beginning to retire, and I'm 60. I have no theatrical training, and I never performed in college. I didn't grow up hoping to become a writer. I have no relevant degrees. I'm 40 years too late."

She listened, then she offered words that would change my life: "Sally, it's *because* you are 60 that you can do this work. You couldn't have done it earlier in your life. *This* is your time." She explained that, in her system, one's sixties were a decade of expansion, not retraction. They were a "yang" time of revitalization and growth.

"That's me, Jean! I feel more inspired, creative, and wiser than ever. Retirement makes no sense."

Why had nobody told me this? What other lies or mistaken concepts about aging was I harboring? Why had I thought that 60 or 70 was the beginning of the end rather than a new opportunity?

According to Jean, I could do things *because* of my age, not *despite* it.

I trembled with excitement as I thanked Jean and hung up. Dancing my way down the gravel path back to the house, I stopped to admire the garden and all that we had created. *How much I love this place and the opportunity to be here!* The honeysuckle and towering Asiatic lilies smelled sweeter than they had an hour earlier. Even the crows seemed to sense my delight and laugh along with me.

My sixties were my take-off, not my landing. I had time.

I wanted to race into the world and say, "Our sixties are the opportunity to express ourselves as never before." Then, I understood a new part of my mission: Since I was a storyteller, I could use my experiences to change society's old, broken, callous, and defeatist narratives about aging. My quest could be an offering, an experiment. I could write and perform what I learned, sharing it with the world to make others' quests a little easier.

As that thought bubbled into my awareness, I felt emboldened. Yes, the road ahead as I aged might not be easy, but if walking it could serve, then it would be worth it. That service would be part of my story—and my joy.

Claiming Age

Seven years later, I proclaimed my message: "Dump denial: 60 is *not* the new 40!" at "Ignite Seattle" by performing it in front of 500 people in a funky, historic theater.

I stepped onto the stage as I heard the master of ceremonies introducing me. I positioned myself on the small red carpet so that a videographer could record my performance. In back of me stood a giant screen that would display my 20 allotted slides. I waited for the audience to hush and took a breath. Once the timer began its five-minute countdown, I dove in.

"How much money do you think gets spent each year globally on "age-defying" and anti-aging products?"

The audience gasped as the answer flashed on a slide: 262 billion dollars. "That's more than the GDP of Portugal."

I heard laughter—the sign that I was off and running.

"All of the stories about aging that I grew up with are wrong." I talked about the myths of retirement, leisure living, and the joke—nursed by some billionaires—that you don't have to age. "I love Twyla Tharp, but just because she can dance vigorously in her eighties doesn't mean you and I will. Unless we happen to have her body and like to get up at five every morning to work it out."

I sensed the audience was with me as I continued. "Ageism is in the air we breathe—and it's crazy. Author Ashton Applewhite calls it 'discriminating against your future self.' You will always carry all of your ages within you, so you don't have to try to be young. Cherish your age."

I told the story of being with Jean Haner, ending it by saying, "Older age is our time to claim our freedom to express ourselves and be who we are."

When the 19th slide flashed behind me, I took a risk. I cried out, "Dump denial!!! Claim your age. On the count of three, shout out your age with me." I screamed, "67!" as the theater exploded into a cacophony of numbers. Slide 20 flashed, and applause filled the space. I danced off the stage, high-fiving my fellow presenters.

During the intermission, I roamed the lobby, sniffing the mix of wine, popcorn, and marijuana scents wafting through the old hall. I was seeking out familiar faces or someone near my age who might have liked my talk when an attractive younger woman wearing ripped designer jeans approached me, wine in hand. She looked about 30, although my ability to judge the ages of people under 40 had diminished. Her face lit up as she said, "I loved your talk! My friends need to hear you—they think life's all downhill after 30. They don't think they have anything to look forward to."

Her friend, a petite brunette, jumped in. "Yeah, my roommate is throwing herself a 30th birthday party and telling everyone to dress in black." A third woman, who had blue-streaked hair and a nose ring, joined in. "My housemate is so depressed about turning *20* because she's convinced that the best years of her life are over."

I was stunned. The need for a new story about aging was greater than I thought.

Facing Fear #1: Money

I didn't need to kill my fears,
I just needed to tame them.
SJF, AGE 67

On stage, I talked about the possibilities aging offered. I didn't mention the fears—such as the three big ones I faced:

~ The fear of running out of money,

~ The fear of losing my health, and

~ The fear of losing my mind.

They weren't without some basis in reality. I'd seen some friends forced to leave their homes for financial reasons, and I'd seen others develop terminal cancer, Parkinson's, and other debilitating diseases. And members of my family had declined or died due to dementia. While some fear seemed justified, I didn't want it running my life. I didn't need to kill it off; I just wanted to tame it.

I decided to tackle my money fears first, hoping to lighten some of the emotional baggage I carried around this issue. It was (and is) embarrassing to have money hang-ups when my life has been one of relative privilege. But my money personality has always been split. On the one hand, I'm a well-educated MBA who can follow investment conversations, understand risk, and analyze economic behavior. On the other hand, I'm still a wounded kid who grew up feeling deprived in the land of the affluent.

As a child, I didn't know how rarefied the air was in our Connecticut suburb, and I grew up tangled in contradictory feelings around money. I knew that my family couldn't afford to buy me the horse I wanted so badly or provide some of the other luxuries my classmates enjoyed. In New Canaan, the affluent paid to send their children to private schools, took foreign vacations, and built architect-designed houses. But, hidden out of view, a percentage spent their afternoons drinking. They denied their teenagers' drug addictions and contemplated suicide. I learned early on that money could not guarantee the happiness, peace, and abundance I wanted.

In contrast, friends in my spiritual community lived on little money, yet their lives appeared rich. But that didn't stop me from being jealous of those who had much more than I did.

One word missing from my early vocabulary was "enough." In New Canaan, the mantra seemed to be, "No matter how much you have, you always need more." Even as a child, I hoped that money might provide a way to ease the sting and shame of loneliness, rejection, and sorrow. As an adult, I knew this wasn't true, yet I still hoped that money might protect me from the pain of someday losing Steve.

That adult, when challenged by household finances or dips in income, could become a frightened, feral child who dropped her fangs in conversation. When Steve tried to allay my fears with his calm, objective reasoning and "We'll be OK" voice, I'd glare at him and respond: "But, what if the economy tanks with the next pandemic? Or you, Steve, become ill and need long-term care? And what if we lose our property in an earthquake?" We do live on a fault line. "And, when you die, who's going to care for me so I don't live my last years alone and destitute?"

Over time, Steve learned that my worries and questions were calls for hugs, not for logical reasoning. I, in turn, learned to notice when my scared child wanted to grab the helm in financial conversations and steer me toward despair.

My fear-taming strategy began with three questions:

1) *How much did Steve and I need to live safely and simply through the end of our lives?* It helped to talk with a financial planner who ran the numbers and evaluated my odds of ending up destitute at the end of my life. (Sociologists have a name for this worry—"bag lady syndrome"—which affects even well-to-do women.) His scenarios helped me understand that, most likely, I'd be OK.

2) *What gave me a feeling of abundance?* Flying back from Tokyo, I felt a sense of plenty that comes from the senses rather than from a bank account. For me, feelings of bountifulness came from tasting a ripe raspberry picked from a prickly vine in summer or dunking my sweating head into cool water. Joy lived in fall colors, burning leaves, and feeling my mare's nose breathing near mine. The more I practiced being present and noticing the world through my senses, the more abundant—and often happier—I was.

3) *What would I do in a "worst case" scenario?* None of us can ensure that the world won't fall apart, especially with the climate in crisis. Yet, I knew I could always draw on my inner strength. In facing a disaster, I would persevere by relying on community, giving to others, and enduring, as people have done across time. Worrying wouldn't help, deepening my faith might.

Even after our conversations with a financial planner, an internal fear storm could still topple me. When it struck, I needed to remember my three questions, have compassion for the scared little girl, and wait for the big waves to subside. It always helped to breathe, meditate, and connect to my body from the inside out. And a creative activity—one as simple as placing a flower in a vase—often helped as well.

Facing Fears #2 and #3:
Losing the Body and the Mind

*M*y list of health woes was growing, but my conditions were nothing compared to what my friends were facing. After all, what's a little osteoporosis, some hearing loss, a few bladder problems . . . OK, I'll stop there!

Good planning could alleviate some of my money worries, but I wasn't so sure it could stop what was happening to my body. Health was beginning to feel like a game of Russian roulette; I never knew when or where I might take the bullet next.

My friend Lynn's situation provided a scary example of this. She was one of the most life-affirming people I'd known. It seemed to me like she had done everything right. She exercised regularly, practiced yoga, and meditated faithfully as a devoted Buddhist. She served her community, supported the marginalized, and exuded positivism. And, she was incredibly kind. But her cancer didn't give a damn. Five months after her diagnosis, she was dead.

Despite my attempts to take care of my health and consume the latest recommended supplements—which I stored in a huge closet pharmacopeia—I still failed to do "healthy living" correctly. In my forties and fifties, I had stayed relatively thin, only to learn that added weight could have strengthened my bones and prevented osteoporosis. I rejected hormone replacement therapy (HRT) during menopause because of the cancer risk, then I learned that it might have decreased my bone loss. Some days, my green tea was on the good list because it was an antioxidant. On other days, it was on the bad list because of its caffeine. (Caffeine is on my list of what I will give up in my next lifetime.) I felt like I couldn't win, and this contributed to my fear. And fear doesn't boost our immune systems.

Luckily, though, I had some healthy habits working for me. My favorite activities, such as walking, singing, being with animals, and taking time in nature, appeared to have sizeable immune system benefits. So, I kept those going. And I read the latest health news and saw my doctor regularly (thank you, Medicare). Beyond that, I prayed.

My third, and perhaps biggest, fear was of losing my mind and memory. I learned that in one study conducted in the United Kingdom, two-thirds of respondents over 50 feared developing dementia, but only one in ten feared getting cancer. I was right there with them. *At least with cancer*, I thought, *there are often treatments*. I found it hard not to worry, at least for a moment, when my mind slipped—like that time when I said "thingy" in a formal speech because the word I needed had gone missing. My husband and I sometimes tag-teamed our sentences, using two heads to come up with a term one of us couldn't remember alone. And there were the times I'd rush into the kitchen or pantry only to wonder, *OK, why am I here?* [Pause. Pause.] *Oh yeah. The mayonnaise.*

From everything I'd read, my experiences were part of the normal aging process. Maybe words were meant to move in and out of my brain, with some taking time off for an occasional vacation. Or perhaps the new words I was learning pushed others out. Often, it was fun to joke about.

Seeing friends descend into actual dementia was not. My artist cousin, Brenda, with her ever-tousled chestnut hair and ever-ready laugh, knew she was a candidate for an early-onset dementia. Multiple women in her family had been afflicted with a non-Alzheimer's form of dementia, and her mom died of it at 64. Brenda received her diagnosis at 49, and she worked to stay upbeat. She kept going with her favorite activities—hiking, painting, and volunteering at her church—as long as she could. Although some say people with Alzheimer's don't suffer because they don't know what they've lost, Brenda always knew what she was losing and what lay ahead.

When Brenda visited me four years before her death, we played together at our island street fair. We danced like fools to an '80s rock-and-roll band, giggled, and strolled down an avenue of merchants peddling clothes, foods, and jewelry. Brenda had always had a bit of the wild-eyed child in her, and I loved how she could strike up a conversation with a stranger. She talked at length with the vendor selling psychedelic tie-dyed T-shirts and eventually bought a purple one from him. The next day, Brenda was delighted to model her new shirt, although she didn't remember her conversation with the man who had sold it to her.

Because of Brenda, I started to learn more about living with dementia. Society often treats people with this condition as outcasts, tragic victims, or our society's version of "untouchables" to be hidden from public view. Brenda was too full of life to deserve any of that (no one does!).

When another favorite relative, Mary, developed Alzheimer's, I visited her in her memory care facility and discovered that my once-shy cousin had become quite social. After years of living alone, she found a boyfriend at the facility. She chattered frankly about her new life without sounding doomed, adding, "I felt so much better about my disease once I learned that getting Alzheimer's wasn't my fault."

In facing the possibility of memory decline, knowing the facts helped. I learned what I could about mental health, the brain, and the realities of dementia. Yet, my fears were unlikely to go away. I faced the challenge of learning to "be with" possibilities I would never want or choose. As I aged, I was learning to walk an existential tightrope between growing fears and new freedom. Holding to the idea of both/and helped enormously.

So did my creative practices. When I was arranging a piece of ike-bana, I didn't have to deny my fears, but I didn't have to focus on them either. Artistic expression gave me a place to put my attention when I found it being pulled into a maelstrom of escalating worry. The joy I felt in publishing a blog post gave me a feeling of agency even in the face of uncertainty and the inevitability of some decline.

Twenty-Eight Steps

Our lives changed when Steve turned 70 and began experiencing heart problems. We had enjoyed hiking earlier in our marriage, but, as walking up hills began to be more of a challenge for him, our days of ascending Northwest mountains appeared to be over. Although I was glad his mind and spirit were staying strong, I didn't enjoy seeing my faithful companion's physical limitations increase as he moved through his 70s.

When Steve was 78, we went on a camping trip to Orcas Island. We thought about climbing scenic Mount Constitution, a small mountain with a fabulous view of Washington's San Juan Islands. But, after some discussion, we decided the uphill was too much for him and opted to walk the trail around the base instead. We set off on a picture-perfect early fall day, blessed with sunshine, a cool breeze, and gorgeous autumn colors. We had been walking for ten minutes when we came to the trail that led to the summit. The path looked loamy, gradual, and tempting. Perhaps, we wondered, if we moved slowly . . .

I didn't want to push Steve, but he wanted to try. I said, "OK. But we'll stop and pause whenever you say so."

That turned out to be about every 28 steps. I'd saunter ahead, counting each one, and then I'd pause to let Steve catch up with me and catch his breath. Each stop became an opportunity for me to study the woods and mentally collect images to write about later. Years earlier, I had done a long hike in the mountains with a boyfriend who paced our progress with his watch. I barely had time to enjoy the views. With Steve, I took in the small delights of the forest. I watched a chipmunk darting about before settling on a stump. He kept a staccato beat going with his tail, a pulse so rhythmic he might have swallowed a metronome. At another stop, I marveled at how moss had covered an entire hillside, carpeting the rocks, stumps, and ground with a chartreuse coating that glowed in the light. I'd walked for years in the Northwest without ever noticing the differences between the barks of two of our common native evergreens. After 30 minutes of hiking with Steve, I knew that the Douglas fir bark had deep, irregular furrows, while the furrows of the western red cedar were striated and vertical.

When we finally reached the summit 90 minutes later, we felt like victorious alpinists. Although we had both ascended much grander peaks in our lives, I remember our hike that day better than any other.

Two months later, I wove my mental images from the walk into a poem for Steve that I called "Twenty-Eight Steps." I presented it to him on his 79th birthday.

The poem hangs on his office wall today, a reminder of my new mantra about aging:

In the face of what I am losing, I am grateful for what I still have.

What Gets Better

After addressing my biggest fears about aging, I still had to deal with the question: *What will give meaning to my life over the next decades as my body declines?* I knew my old go-tos—achievement and ambition—wouldn't help me play the long haul.

I read everything I could about aging. Books on retirement that touted new terms such as "rewirement" or "refirement" had begun appearing, offering ways to change careers or start volunteering. Such books endorsed the idea of engagement and following our passions. Yet, I was suspicious that they were just offering a way to keep living our lives as we always had—with less work and more time off for good behavior. Was rewirement just a guise to support our societal obsession with material success and ambition—this time for folks over 50? Or was this time our opportunity to find "more"?

I saw friends jump from full-time employment into consulting contracts that offered them a way to stay busy and stimulated—and forestall the void left after leaving a job. One of them made a comment that rang true for me: "I feel like I still have to earn the right to do nothing."

Why do we have to earn that right? Will just "being" ever be enough for us?

I discovered authors I loved—mostly philosophers, psychologists, and spiritual teachers—who provided some of the insight about aging

I sought. Dr. Thomas Moore offered me a way to embrace the complex feelings that can come with age and enjoy new freedom to follow the Muse and create. The late psychologist and geriatrician Dr. Gene Cohen suggested that we might become even more creative as we age. In *The Mature Mind,* he used his research findings to assert: "Contrary to societal myths, creativity is hardly the exclusive province of youth. It can blossom at any age—and in fact it can bloom with more depth and richness in older adults because it is informed by their vast stores of knowledge and experience."

That certainly rang true for me. I'd never felt as creatively alive as I had post-midlife. And the women over 60 who filled my ikebana and writing classes appeared to be having similar experiences. They, too, seemed intent on developing new parts of their creative selves that might have lain dormant for years.

I took comfort in the words of the Franciscan Father Richard Rohr, whose writings helped me make sense of my experiences. When I first read his book, *Falling Upward,* I was 56 and confused about my desire to let go of parts of my career and ways of being. His words suggested that my life's first and second halves were designed to be different and that I wasn't crazy to be feeling a change. In life's first half, he wrote, we build ourselves up and create an infrastructure. In the second half, we take apart some of what we built and let go of the objects, attachments, and identities we once depended on. Fifteen years later, I read Jungian psychologist Dr. Connie Zweig's description of something similar: She wrote about aging as moving "from role to soul."

In my twenties, I studied the work of the Austrian educator Rudolf Steiner and felt drawn to his fourfold typology of the human being as mind, body, soul, and spirit. I knew I had a soul and envisioned it as the source of my imagination, intuition, and creative spark. As I saw it, after midlife, my job was to nourish that soul. My spirit felt harder to define, yet tremendously important, as it connected me to a greater

Spirit and the spiritual reality of the universe. I experienced it in my yearning for the Divine, in my awe watching the birth of a foal, or in a piece of music that lifted me toward the numinous.

For Steiner, the presence of a spiritual world was a fact that could be studied scientifically. I lacked his clarity and enormous knowledge, yet I'd always felt there was more to life than this material reality. When I felt the depth of my Longing, life extended far beyond what I could understand. I suspected support and guidance from spiritual worlds might be available to me if I could figure out how to tap into it.

While my cosmology of the afterlife was pretty sketchy, I trusted Steiner's wisdom that our spirits did continue after death. Of course, I had no proof for this; yet it made sense to me.

Although my ruminations might have sounded philosophical to some, I considered them to be very practical. My body was going to decline—that was a given—and my mind might as well. But my soul and spirit could continue to expand if I nurtured them.

As I thought about aging, I saw a landscape fraught with complexity. I hoped that any encounters with pain, although not desired, would season me and build my compassion. My own mortality was on the horizon, and I had been seasoned by loss. Creativity and imagination had become lights that were helping illuminate the way ahead.

The words "both/and" stayed with me whenever I thought about the decades to come. Life could get better, *and* it could still be incredibly tough. Aging could bring losses *and* gifts. Among the gifts were:

~ I was happier with my appearance than in my late twenties.

~ I kept learning new words, spurred on by my desire to write.

~ The intuitive part of my mind was blossoming.

~ I noticed more details in nature, even in our backyard.

~ I had wisdom to offer my clients based on my experience (if not my tech expertise!).

~ I could experience time more fully.

~ I could let go of some false ideas about myself.

~ I could release the idea that I'd ever be perfect or transformed.

~ I felt less need to achieve and more delight in what I created.

~ I was less angry and more grateful.

Aging well didn't require facelifts, tummy tucks, or the illusion that life would always work out. Aging would bring difficulties, *and* I would have opportunities to express myself more freely and authentically. The new story about aging I was discovering was big enough to hold the both/and-ness of life. It spoke of feeding my soul and gaining new freedom to create. It reminded me to listen to the whispers and support that came through both gentle nudges and a presence I would soon call the Muse.

Meeting the Muse

Enter the Muse

I'm not here to channel spirits into bestsellers. I'm here
to support you. And I'm really quite ordinary.
Isabel

Twelve years into my post-midlife journey, I met the Muse.

Before I describe our first encounter, let me share a disclaimer. I'm not psychic. I've never been clairvoyant, clairaudient, or clair-anything. I'm a feet-on-the-ground MBA with a strong sense of intuition. But I've always known, in my heart of hearts, that there's more to life than meets the eye.

On the night of our meeting, my good friend Rondi and I had gathered to practice the traditional Tibetan art of "toning"—singing beautiful sounds with multi-octave overtones. We lit a sole candle to set the mood in the darkened room. Rondi was more successful at achieving overtones, a technique that turned out to be above my pay grade. Still, as I explored different notes, my head filled with sound, and a delightful buzz pulsed through my body.

After our 40-minute sonic workout, Rondi and I sat in silence with our eyes closed. I planted my feet on the ground to allow the waves of sensation to travel from my head to my toes. Then, in the middle of this vibration-fest, I sensed a presence to my left, like a dense cloud of energy but with a shape. No one had entered the room, yet some force was clearly present.

With my eyes still shut, I saw a woman in her late eighties with lustrous white skin, glowing pearl-gray eyes, and silver hair. Her head was tipped slightly forward, and her body looked shortened by age. When she smiled, her eyes twinkled. I immediately wanted to know her and launched a silent conversation while Rondi sat quietly meditating.

"Thank you for coming," I began. "It's late now, but I'd like to know more about you. Would you be willing to join me first thing tomorrow morning for a chat?"

Although I couldn't be sure, the warm feeling I received made me think she agreed. After sitting for a few more minutes in her presence, I opened my eyes and returned to the room. I didn't say anything to Rondi about my experience; I simply thanked her for the toning session and said goodbye as she left.

The following day, I couldn't wait to meet my new friend. I had invited her to join me in the place I reserved for writing, contemplation, and reading—a small cabin 80 feet from our back door. Every morning that I could I went there, often before the sun rose, to meditate before being swept into other work. My cabin seemed like the perfect spot for my first conversation with the Muse.

I walked the gravel path to my retreat space holding a steamy cup of green tea in one hand and my computer in the other. When I walked in, I flicked on the room's soft amber lights and nestled into my old blue recliner. I opened my laptop, pictured the being I had seen the night before and waited. Almost immediately, she appeared.

"I am so happy to be with you, my dear," she said. *"And, how nice that you made tea. Shall we have a little together?"* Tea, it turned out, was a shared passion, and sipping a cup would become the ritual that launched our conversations.

"Thank you so much for coming," I said. "I'm so happy to know you. But . . . could you please tell me who you are? I mean, like, are you a spirit? Are you here to help me channel messages?" (I was thinking of the New Age authors who'd made a fortune writing spirit-guided texts.)

"Oh, no, no, my darling. I don't want to disappoint you, but that's not me. I'm not here to channel spirits into bestsellers. I'm here to support you. And I'm really quite ordinary."

Too bad, I joked to myself, I wasn't going to be able to offer the world some all-knowing message coming from other realms. But something about Isabel suggested we were going for more—a friendship. Her "voice" sounded light and pleasant.

"Do you have a name?" I asked and waited. The word "Isabel" popped right up, and I tried it out. "Would it be all right if I called you Isabel?"

"Oh yes, that would be fine, indeed. I rather like Isabel."

"Would you mind if I type your words when we talk?"

"Not at all. In fact, that would be a very good idea. Take your time and tell me when your computer is ready."

"I'm good. Could we talk about where I seem to be going in life?" I sensed that she already knew about the path I was on, even though we hadn't spoken about it.

"Oh yes, that's part of why I'm here. To support you on this creative path you're walking. But I won't tell you what to do. Believe me, I'm not a prophet. I do have good sense of joy and what makes us come alive, and I want to support that in you."

Hearing her interest in my creative work and not knowing how else to label her, I decided to call her my Muse. Isabel seemed fine with this.

"The words don't really matter, my dear, as much as our relationship."

With my computer open on my lap, I transcribed everything she was saying. I tried not to put words into her mouth, although, realistically, I probably did. Or was her mouth my mouth? Perhaps it was, although she often offered perspectives that weren't tainted by my fears, sadness, or other emotions. At the same time, she always showed compassion for whatever I was going through. I turned to her when I was upset by a conflict with a friend, worried about where I was going, or stuck in a piece of writing. Her words were often simple.

"Oh, my dear. I can see you are hurting. These kinds of conflicts are quite hard. I hope things will resolve with your friend. It may just take time and hurt for a while—hurts are always part of being human. So, today, could you give yourself a little comfort? Could you stop for a moment to feel the love that is there for you? We love you so much. (She often used "we.")

"I think it could help you to connect with your wonderful land. Why not take a little walk and go talk with your tree?"

We shared a love of trees.

I didn't always follow her suggestions, but whenever I did, I felt renewed and grateful.

The Muses in History

After we met, I started to research Muses. None of the ones I read about had appeared on a wave of vibratory energy. The most famous Muses were the nine Greek goddesses, daughters of Zeus and Mnemosyne, the Titan goddess of memory. Each of the Muses was responsible for inspiring a different aspect of Greek art and culture, including the sciences. The Greeks could recognize a Muse by the object she carried, such as a writing tablet (Calliope, Muse of epic poets) or lyre (Terpsichore, Muse of dancers). I found the Greek Muses a bit dusty, if fascinating. They were more prone to sit atop a marble hall than drop into a studio for a visit.

I also read about famous human Muses. Often, they were the lovers of poets or artists, like the brilliant Lou Andreas-Salomé, paramour of Rainer Marie Rilke. She eventually dumped him as a lover but continued to support him throughout his writing career. Artists Frida Kahlo and Diego Rivera were Muses to each other but in decidedly stormy ways. And, some Muses were objects of unrequited love, as in the case of W.B. Yeats' obsession with Maud Gonne. After observing the complexity of these very human relationships, I questioned the merit of making your Muse your lover. Luckily, I didn't think this was going to be an issue with Isabel.

Author Elizabeth Gilbert, in her popular and inspiring TED Talk called "Your Elusive Creative Genius," spoke about the Muse as an unseen deliverer of great ideas—a force that can blow into town, seemingly out of nowhere, then disappear. While I loved her reverence for the Muse, I preferred mine to be more reliable.

I struggled to understand who Isabel was during our first years together. Her voice sometimes sounded a bit like mine, so I wondered if she was perhaps a vehicle of my imagination or a conduit for my intuition. Yet, there were times she surprised me with an insight I hadn't thought of—at least consciously—and I wondered if she might exist in some subtle transpersonal realm.

I turned to David Spangler, a friend and teacher who had years of experience communicating with subtle presences and beings. At a weekend retreat, I caught up with him during a break and asked, "Do you think my Muse is just a part of my imagination, or might she also be a subtle being?"

David smiled warmly and, with his characteristic chuckle, said, "Yes." I laughed, enjoying David's wit as well as his wisdom. Even though this was not the definitive answer I'd hoped for, it seemed perfect.

For David, communicating with subtle presences and energies was a fact of life and not at all exotic. Because he saw the sacred in every individual and in all of life, including nature and the cosmos, he didn't view subtle spiritual beings as rarefied or special. For him, they were collaborators—potential partners in making the planet a healthy and holy place to live. He wanted nothing to do with the glamour that surrounded some spiritual teachers. He preferred to be, like Isabel, ordinary.

David's comments helped me to stop worrying about who Isabel might be. I didn't have to know as long as I felt like she was helping me. And, I began to see that I'd probably always been guided by a Muse-like force, if you count the whispers and intuitions I'd received over the years. The seven-year-old me received clues like, *"Why not follow this deer path today?"* My 20-something self received more career-focused suggestions. One told me to go to business school, even when that sounded like an outlandish idea. After I graduated with my MBA, I heard an inner voice telling me to go west to Seattle. Even though such hints changed my life, I never considered their sources.

By the time I reached my sixties, the guidance I was receiving was subtler—more like wisps of wind, feelings in my heart, hunches that just appeared. When I shaped flowers in ikebana class, I learned to follow these gentle suggestions. *"Choose this vase today. Trim half the leaves from this camellia branch. Add another flower."* Such small messages were guiding my creative life. Maybe I needed them as much as—or more than—the more directive announcements I'd received at times in the past. I was slowly learning to listen, hear, and act, and then check out what happened—without having to be sure of what I was doing.

Maybe the Muse had waited to appear until she was sure that I'd listen and receive what she could give.

I'd always closeted my interest in subtle and spiritual worlds when I was around people who seemed uninterested in such matters—the ones who might have laughed at me in business school. In those days, credibility and fitting in seemed all important. But in my sixties, the world looked different.

I thought about my experience with my beloved springer spaniel, Lady, who'd passed some years before. Like most dogs, she had an incredible nose. If she could have talked, she might have asked me, her deficient human, "Do you smell that delicious scent of decaying rat down the road?" Then, I would have been forced to admit, "I don't know what you're talking about—I don't smell a thing." But the fact that I couldn't smell the rat with my limited nose-powers didn't mean that such fetid splendor didn't exist. I just didn't have the senses needed to detect it. Now, instead of cowering when someone didn't understand my relationship with the spiritual or subtle worlds, I could tell myself we had different noses or ways of perceiving. As I moved toward 70, wasn't it time to stop hiding my desire to see into and understand the invisible, mysterious dimensions of life? Why be deterred by what others thought?

If connecting with the Muse was just a way to exercise my imagination . . . well, so be it. My explorations seemed to help my creativity. I wasn't denying rationality. I was enhancing it with intuition—another case of both/and.

Talking with the Muse

*Love draws us to you. If the only thing we do together
is to expand the love you feel for yourself and the
world around you—and then help you receive the
love that is available for you—we'd be happy.*
—Marco (Muse)

Whenever I wanted to converse with Isabel, all I needed to do was sit in my writing cabin with a cup of tea for us and ask for help. Soon, I'd hear her words and type them as fast as I could, using a process similar to what some call "automatic writing"—letting words roll through in a stream of consciousness. That label seemed close to a description of our conversations, although nothing felt "automatic" about them. I felt more like I was talking with a friend—a friend with a personality.

Her suggestions helped me when I was overwhelmed or discouraged:

"How can you make this task ahead of you more pleasurable?"
"Where might you bring a little beauty into your life right now?"

She knew I struggled with self-judgment and comparison. When my ferocious inner gremlins cried, *"Your work is not good enough,"* she coached me. *"Keep loving what you are doing. That's all you need."*

When I asked her, "Am I crazy to be doing this?" she replied, *"You know you're not, so don't go there."*

When I was despondent and unsure, she'd say, *"Trust your Longing. You judge yourself harshly, my dear. I want you to enjoy what you're doing and know it's OK to be you. Follow your desire and create what inspires you. The journey you're on may not make sense to you, but it doesn't have to. Can you enjoy it anyway?"*

She often suggested taking micro-steps as a path out of my occasional despair. *"What step could you take in the next five minutes that would feel good? Calling your mother? Or weeding the peas?"*

Over the next couple of years, Isabel and I came to know each other so well that I could almost anticipate what she would say. Her thoughts about self-compassion, taking opportunities for pleasure, letting go of self-judgment, and delighting in creative work lived in my heart.

At that point, a couple of other Muses began visiting. One was more of a philosopher and a bit of a poet as well. Sometimes he reminded me of the late Irish poet John O'Donohue, whose words never failed to inspire. I called this new Muse "Marco." He tried to explain the role of the Muses, saying:

> *"We are here to strengthen you. You do not have to 'believe in us,' and we want no blind followers. Your job is to always test what we offer and think things through. And to remember that the capacities and truths you need are already living in you. We can help you with that."*

Marco also helped me think about how to describe the Muse to others who might have or want to have relationships with personified Muses or subtle presences. I furiously wrote down his words when he said:

> *"Another way to think about the Muse is as a gateway to the intuition and imagination. Lots of forms of guidance are available to people—and not just via presences with personalities. People*

may experience the Muse as 'a heightened sense of inner knowing,' 'a way of listening to the world that does not speak,' or 'a tuning into the flow of life.' However people experience guidance, the process is the same. It always involves listening, receiving, appreciating, reflecting, and acting."

His words helped broaden my definition of a Muse.

And still, I found it useful, comforting, and inspiring to be able to converse with a presence, especially when the world felt dark. That presence reassured me, like Marco did when he offered this support:

"We love you very much and feel your love. Love draws us to you. Love lives at the foundation of our relationships. If the only thing we do together is to expand the love you feel, both for yourself and for the world around you—and then help you receive the love that is available for you—we'd be happy.

"There are times, we know, that you'd like specific answers about how to get clients or revise your website, and I wish that we could give them to you. But we aren't all knowing, although we can help you find questions to ask. Sometimes, we may offer ideas, but the journey is always yours. If you stumble on self-doubt, need reinforcement, or forget who you are, we can help.

"Not everyone believes in Muses or cares about them, and that doesn't matter. Trust your experiences."

I thought of how David Spangler had ended our brief conversation. He'd made one last comment: "Keep going, and learn from your experiences, my friend."

Letting Go

Calling My Bluff

Walking a creative path challenges the parts of us that want to cling and know. But to make art or life, we must let go and risk the unknown. As we expand, we move beyond who we thought we were into the deeper current of who we are. We allow the wild possibility that lives within to pull us toward the future.

As we walk through the land of liminality, we may feel raw, tired, anxious, and lost as the horizon of our known world disappears from view. Yet, if we listen, we may be blessed to hear a chorus of angels cheering for our becoming.
—MARCO

I spent hours in my cabin chair chatting with Isabel as I grappled with how to describe myself on my first website. I'd write my best, consultant-sounding description of myself or my services, only to delete the copy a few months later when I couldn't stand the artificial tone of my voice.

"*Be kind,*" said Isabel. "*Who you are is still becoming. Let this website be your experiment.*"

A few months earlier, I'd sensed that I needed to prepare for change. My government contract for the leadership program that I had run for 21 years was coming up for renewal, and its continuation was not guaranteed. I would need to compete for the work by bidding and writing a proposal as I'd done many times before. *Do I want another three-year round?* I wondered. *How many years will I keep teaching leadership when so many new creative projects are calling to me?*

When I first won the contract at 42, I loved directing the program. I'd been thrilled by the opportunity to design a leadership program outside of the one I ran for the university. But after 9/11, the mood in the agency I'd worked with became increasingly autocratic, and the collaborative, participative style of management I espoused no longer fit them well. The executives who originally hired and supported me had retired, and the woman managing my contract at the time wasn't my biggest fan. Still, the work provided most of my income, and I couldn't imagine letting it go.

There's a scene in the movie *Wild* where the hero, Cheryl Strayed, begins her solo hike along the Pacific Crest Trail. She has packed so much that she can barely lift her backpack. A veteran hiker makes her go through her pack and give up everything that is not essential—which turns out to be a lot.

I understood, at least theoretically, that the aging process often ushers in the need to let go—of stuff, of work, of what we once could do, and, often, of our identities. But, like Strayed, I couldn't lighten my load without help. When the time came to bid on the contract, I cringed as I read the government's 140-page "Request for Proposal." I had written many of these, so I knew the process would require a month's work.

Isabel and Marco stepped in to challenge me. They asked, *"What does your heart say? Is this what you want to be doing?"*

I negotiated with myself. *I'll find a way to design the program so it will be creative and fun again.* I added new ideas into the proposal, which Steve helped me edit, and I made sure I addressed all the requirements. Then, I submitted what we thought was a first-rate document.

While I was awaiting the bid results, I developed a painful case of "frozen shoulder" that limited how I could use my right arm. I had no clue what had provoked it, and, according to the doctor, there was no cure besides giving it time to "melt"—the term for when the shoulder unlocks and the pain decreases. Later, as I read more about the body, I learned that frozen shoulder can be triggered by high-stress situations in which the body is being told to stop and go forward at the same time. That was my reality: I was trying to move forward in my life while not knowing if I'd have any work. The agency had told me I'd have their decision within a month. But one month stretched into two, then three, then four. As the start of the new program year approached, I felt optimistic, but I had no news.

During that period of unknowing, the time came for me to attend an eight-day storytelling workshop in Santa Fe with actor-director Tanya Taylor Rubinstein. I'd signed up to take her "Story Healers" certification program nine months earlier, wanting to learn to coach others to present their stories on stage. When I finally boarded the flight to New Mexico, I was tingling with anticipation and barely able to sit still in my seat.

I arrived too late at night to view the garden surrounding the one-room adobe casita I had rented. But the next morning, a wash of golden sun woke me up as it flooded the room. I went to the window and saw yucca, succulents, cacti, and prairie primroses growing in the parched red earth. New energy stirred in me as I beheld the beauty of this world—spikey and dry, so different from what I had come from in the lush Pacific Northwest.

With an hour to go before my scheduled ride to the workshop, I meditated, fixed tea and hot cereal, and opened my computer to check a few emails. One jumped out at me from a former competitor for the consulting contract. In its subject line, I read, "Sorry you didn't win." I stared at the screen blankly without understanding.

Then I did. The woman monitored government contracts and must have read online that I had lost. My heart pounded. *She has to be wrong.*

How could I have lost? My proposal was first-rate, as always. I was meant to win. I raced to the government's contracting webpage and saw another firm's name listed as the winning bidder.

I rose to call Steve when my head started spinning. I grabbed the phone and sat down before I keeled over. My years of agency work were over, and my income was gone. Yes, I had been ambivalent about it, but that didn't mean I wanted them to reject me. Shaking, I called Steve. "Honey, I lost the contract."

He paused, then calmly said, "I'm sorry. How could that be? Your bid was so good."

"I don't know. It's over, and I don't even care. If you want to know, you can check it out."

"OK, I will." He added a preemptive, "I know you're worried about the money. We'll be fine."

I stared out the window as a goldfinch feasted on a thistle. While it pecked away, I realized that I wasn't entirely sad. Disappointed, yes; but also excited that this loss could be an opening to the creative time I'd been craving.

My husband called back. "The other firm's price proposal was less than two-thirds of yours."

Aha. Low-balling.

The firm might have been willing to cut fees or take a loss to get its foot in the government's door. I couldn't run the program for that price. But it didn't matter. I was done.

A car honked, and I hung up the phone. Twenty minutes later, I was nestled in a plush cream couch at Tanya's, surrounded by four other women writer-storytellers. I sipped my tea as Tanya invited us to share what had brought us to the workshop. Each of my classmates spoke, and I listened calmly until it was my turn. Then, it was as if a tsunami of emotion hit, and I burst into sobs.

So much for being detached about my loss.

The women soon surrounded me with hugs, and I melted into their kindness.

My new life is starting—and this is my new tribe.

At 6 am, a door to my life had snapped shut. At 9 am, another opened. Life had called my bluff. I said I wanted more time to create. At age 63, I now had it.

Story Healing

*Use your wound to create. Composers, performers,
artists, and writers do that. Find the beauty
wherever you are and say "yes" to life.*
—MARCO

Tanya knew how much healing is possible when difficult stories are shared in front of others. She wanted the four of us in training with her to experience her process before we coached others. During our first week, we crafted pieces to present on a Santa Fe stage that weekend.

She taught us to embody our words, drawing from her training. As I practiced a scene about working in the garden in front of the others, Tanya called out directions: "Show it to us," "Feel it in your body," "Let us feel you."

Improvising on the spot, I imagined a heavy spade in my hand, a hot midday sun in the sky, and beads of sweat pouring off my back. Bugs circled near me, and I used my dirty hand to push them away and wipe the snot off my nose. In front of my classmates, I dug an imaginary hole wide enough for a tree and deep enough to hold my purpose. I practiced describing my work in the garden and the shock and humiliation I had felt after losing my big contract.

When the Saturday night performance rolled around, I could feel the 200-member audience supporting me with their laughter, sighs, and silence. In being witnessed and heard, the load of shame I had been carrying about losing the contract lightened. I took a bow after eight minutes and left the stage beaming, feeling charged up about my new life as a story coach, performer, and writer. I'd lost a job but won what I most wanted: time to explore new parts of myself and to create.

Giving Up a Professional Identity

*We are all creators, pulled forward by the faint call of
our next assignment. Walking a creative path challenges
the part of us that has to know where we are going.
But to create art or life, we have to risk the unknown.
A cold wind invigorates as the angels cheer.*
—MARCO

*B*ack on the island, I pursued my passion for storytelling. Some days, I felt blessed to have more time for writing and creating. On other days, my lack of income freaked me out.

More than money, I'd lost an identity when I'd lost that contract. When people at parties asked me what I did, I mumbled something about "a creative path" and "storytelling coaching." That's when they usually headed off to eat more olives.

The truth was, I still needed time to know where I was going. I was traveling in the land of the liminal—the in-between zone where you can't see the horizon and have to sight on vague visions, hunches, and desires. I knew where I'd been, but my goals for what was ahead were still fuzzy.

The difficulty I had in expressing my direction hit home when my friend Margaret visited that fall. Margaret was a favorite professional friend who had heard me perform at the polarity thinking conference. She was one of the earliest boosters of my storytelling and wanted to see me take my performances out into the world. I looked forward to telling her about my new discoveries and consulting aspirations. And, I'd hoped she'd share some of her marketing wisdom, as she always seemed to have a full fleet of consulting clients who valued her feet-on-the-ground approach to developing their businesses.

We began walking down my street toward the Point Robinson Lighthouse as Mount Rainier offered us one of its rare cloudless appearances. The remaining golden leaves in a grove of quaking aspens rustled in the breeze. Margaret talked about her full workload, which she hoped to start cutting back.

When we arrived at the beach, we nestled into two long, white driftwood logs. I scanned the waters, hoping an orca might pass by, but none were swimming through neighborhood waters that day. Margaret spoke a little more, then paused and asked about my work. I rambled about island living, creativity, gardening, storytelling, and my transitions. Then my tone of voice changed, and I flipped into marketing mode. I said, "I want to tell stories and promote my leadership storytelling to organizations. Do you have any ideas for me?"

A tiny gray shore crab scooted by my leg.

Margaret's answer was not what I expected. "I don't see how you're going to develop professionally when you're living on an island."

My breath shortened, and I felt sucker-punched. I didn't think to ask Margaret what she meant. Years later, she would tell me she had intended her comment as a compliment—"I see you as a gifted performer, which is why I think you need to be in New York or a major city." But I didn't hear any of that because the crescendo of criticism from the gremlins proved deafening.

"Margaret is a friend and a supporter. If she can't understand what you're doing, who will? Frankly, the world will never get you. Or see you as valuable. Plus, you're here, off-track and lost."

Feeling weakened by their assault, I had no voice to describe how life on our new property was feeding my soul. I wasn't just living on an island—the island was living in me. I wasn't just seeding my property—I was fertilizing a seed in me. Sure, I was putting hours into the garden to prepare for being on the Vashon Island Garden Tour. But gardening inspired me, and I had started chronicling my new obsession in short essays. And, no, I couldn't articulate where I was going, but I was finding my way a step at a time.

The gremlins, though, were relentless. *"Don't kid yourself. You'll never again be professionally successful if you continue spending your time like this."*

As Margaret and I walked up the hill back to the house, I sank into shame, babbling a few words to conceal my feelings. Lost in an emotional riptide, I didn't see that I had set Margaret up. I had asked for concrete guidance when I was still trying to dream what I wanted.

The following day, after we said goodbye, I ran to my bedroom and collapsed on the floor. I sat staring blankly at our small pond where the robins were skinny-dipping in the cold water. Even the dat-dat-dat sound of a woodpecker making its home in the snag of a madrona tree didn't cheer me up. Steve came in, saw me sprawled on the carpet, and asked, "What's wrong?"

"Margaret didn't get what I was doing. At all. I'm not valuable. At all. What I'm doing is crazy."

Steve raised his eyebrows and continued to stare at me. He'd heard too many variations of this tune.

"I feel like I'm losing my professional identity!" I thought this was code for, "Big hug, please."

But Steve broke into guffaws. "A professional identity. What the hell is that?"

That was *not* what I wanted to hear, and I glared at him. All I saw was kindness, even as he continued to roar. Finally, infected by his mirth, I started chuckling and quickly melted into full-body, shake-my-insides laughter. I saw the joke. I'd been telling Steve about Richard Rohr's ideas on letting go of the grip of our egos in the second half of life. Yet, I'd been desperately holding on to mine, thinking I still had to *be* someone in the eyes of the world.

I held my aching belly as Steve extended his hand to me. "You're doing the right thing," he said as he gently pulled me up.

Emptying the Files

No one throws you a going-away party when you work for yourself. After I lost my government contract, there was no celebration. There weren't even any thank-yous. The contract administrator emailed me a request to return my access key card immediately, and we were done. I left my teaching materials stuffed in a large filing cabinet in my office, untouched.

Six years later, at age 68, the pandemic provided a needed opportunity to sort and purge my belongings. I went through my clothes, pulling out the professional outfits I might never wear again and making piles to give away. Then, I tackled the attic, where I continued the process of letting go as I sifted through outdated art supplies, fabric, and cheap picture frames I'd never use. Then, I hit a roadblock: our once-valuable camping equipment.

Are we ready to admit we'll never take another long backpacking trip?

That felt too painful and I decided I wasn't quite ready to let our supplies go. (Alas, the stuff is still up there, and it still needs to go.)

Finally, I attacked the professional files. I foraged through the four-drawer vertical cabinet, stumbling upon course designs, workbooks, newspaper clippings of articles I had written, marketing brochures, photos of students, and articles about leadership.

Occasionally, I stopped to read a letter from a student or a testimonial—taking time to remember the clients I'd deeply cared about and those who told me that I had changed their lives. I thought back through my projects, especially the ones that had challenged and inspired me. Some of my work had felt like a gift from the gods, such as the contract in Japan, a storytelling project with a health care system, and an assignment in India.

A wave of melancholy rolled in as I realized I wasn't just saying goodbye to a file cabinet full of documents; I was saying goodbye to a career. I hadn't built a consulting empire, but that was never my goal. Sure, I had a few regrets—little wounds and scars that came out of 40 years of work. But, I'd helped people, and I'd supported my life with a respectable and engaging practice.

After four hours in my office, the remains of 30 years of consulting work rested in two oversized file folders. Three large trash barrels held paper ready for recycling. I looked at the four empty drawers and said, "Thank you."

I had begun to let go of stuff I didn't need.

Now, it was time to also dispense with some outdated ideas and behaviors, many of which related to my relationship with my body.

Finding the Body . . . Beautiful

Heeding the Signs

Five days after I moved to New York City at age 26, I saw a revolver pointed directly at my heart. "Give me your purse," the man said, as I stood on a dark street quaking, my feet frozen to the sidewalk. I handed him my purse with my glasses and all of my money, and I watched him take off into the night. As soon as he'd disappeared, I thought, *There was something weird about that man, and I didn't listen.*

When I got back to my cousin's house in Brooklyn where I was staying and finally stopped shaking, I thought about the scene and the warning signs I had overlooked. I had gone to a nearby convenience store to buy yogurt and had noticed a man wandering about checking out the aisles and freezers. He did a lot of looking, yet he only bought a small carton of milk and a Twinkie. My body had broadcast warnings through a tightened chest and queasy stomach—it knew I was being cased. Ignoring the message, I purchased an apple and a container of yogurt and left the premises to walk home alone. Moments after I turned the corner, that same man threatened my life.

I told myself I would never blow off my body's advice like that again. I began to listen more carefully to how and when my it spoke to me. Danger felt like a quickening heart or a foreboding stirring in my gut. A slight internal shiver could mean I was about to receive an insight. My Longing surfaced through a swelling in my chest or at the back of my throat. A deep calm or impending tears accompanied experiences of beauty or the Divine. And, when I was working on a project, like a bed in the garden, a warmth in my heart often meant, *"Do that."*

In my sixties, my body would become a key ally when I created—the lightening rod through which Spirit could pour into my imagination. But in order for it to become a creative conduit, I had to stop pushing first.

Push-a-Holic

As a child, I loved staying busy. When I was in my mid-twenties, living in Manhattan's Upper West Side, I took busyness to the next level. I became a push-a-holic, committed to packing as many experiences and adventures as possible into a 24-hour day. After all, I was in the "City That Never Sleeps," so I considered rest discretionary. I overdosed on work, cultural opportunities, exercise, and friends. Every Sunday, I'd sweat while reading *The New York Times* entertainment section, lamenting the many cultural events I'd never be able to attend.

One particularly packed Saturday, I rose at 6 am and headed for my daily run around Central Park, enjoying fewer crowds while the mist still covered the lake. After returning to my apartment, I showered, gobbled a muffin, and walked ten blocks south to a class called "Spiritual Approaches to Color." Then, it was off to see a naturopath, followed by lunch with a friend at an Upper West Side café. I said goodbye to her and scooted across Central Park to see the magnificent Tutankhamun exhibit at the Metropolitan Museum of Art. I gawked at the treasured golden and obsidian funeral mask and viewed as many crowns, coffins, and pieces of jewelry as I could in the limited time I had. But with a play to see that evening, I had to leave after two hours and dash back to my apartment. There, I grabbed snacks and changed my clothes. I ran down a flight of stairs to the street, hailed a taxi, collapsed in the back seat, and watched the city lights rush past me in a blur. Only then did I think, *What am I doing? What's the use of doing so much if I'm not even there?*

In my defense, I was living in a culture that thrived on hyperproductivity and counting accomplishments, even in one's "free time." In Manhattan, everyone seemed to rush, so my addiction went unnoticed. Living alone, I felt chronically lonely, and busyness provided some relief. Like an addict, I used checking accomplishments and cultural events off my to-do list as a fix.

Fast-forward to an international career with many assignments abroad, a trip to business school, a subsequent career in education, and doctoral studies. As I handed in my dissertation at age 42, I could feel my energy sputtering out. I complained to a doctor who told me that a woman's adrenal system was designed for bodies that rarely lived past 40. No wonder my reserve tank was gone.

Yet, I still felt almost powerless to stop pushing. It would take an intervention to get me to listen to my body's wisdom.

Befriending the Body

The body is always present.
The mind is a time traveler.
—ANONYMOUS

"*Stop the crazy talk,*" I heard my Muses—or, at that point, mysterious guiding voices—tell me when I was 26. I'd been basking in the glow of my new figure, appreciating how, for the first time in my life, I was the skinny ideal woman I'd always hoped to be. I'd gotten very sick on a work assignment in Mali, and my weight dropped from 124 pounds to 104 pounds. My unidentified illness and the dysentery that came along with it had been painful—but what a reward!

I twirled in front of the mirror and admired my shape. *Great butt.* As I celebrated my look in pants, I tried to not notice that the bones in my arms had started to stick out. I continued celebrating my weight loss until my gremlin voice started taunting, "*It's not enough. Your stomach still sticks out. You should lose just a little more—to be safe.*"

Thankfully, that day my good guides cried, "*Enough!*" and yanked me away from the edge of anorexia. "*No more weighing yourself—ever!*" I snapped out of the trance I'd been in and gave them my word. (I've kept my promise for 40 years.)

Without knowing it, I'd fallen victim to a disease that affected a lot of women with whom I grew up: the idea that you could control your life if you controlled your weight. The problem with this thinking, I found, is that *controlling* a life isn't a very good way to *have* a life. When I moved to Seattle at age 32, I gave away the size 4 clothes I'd kept from my New York years and settled into both a size 8 and a happier life.

When I stopped trying to force my body into some externalized image of what it was supposed to be, I also started to listen to it. Truthfully, I had to. I'd blown my reserve tank and my body became the de facto no-bullshit arbitrator of how much I could do. By the time I turned 60, I couldn't overdo anything without the risk of falling into a funk. That meant no more late-night projects, 11 pm dance parties, red-eye flights, or weeks of adrenalized work.

My body's constraints frustrated me when I worked in the garden. Twinges from my wrists warned me to stop as I tried to eliminate the 572 shot weeds, 57 native blackberry vines, 42 buttercups, and 778 sticky weeds that had come in with the evening's rain.

I'd negotiate. *"How much more time can I weed?"*

My wrists would reply: *"Twenty minutes. Or else."*

If I violated their terms, I could count on a night of agony, with pains shooting from my elbows to my numb fingertips. My vulnerabilities seemed unfair; a slight stumble on a root could trigger a week of limping. My body was a demanding teacher whose punishments often felt unduly harsh.

I disliked the limitations that came with being 60, but I would never choose to go back to age 26. Instead, I wanted to work with what I could still do with my body, and in the process, see how it might inform my imagination and my soul.

Wild-Eyed

Despite pushing my body too much, I'd always loved moving it, starting with the days I used to gallop around my childhood house in New Canaan. In improv classes, my favorite exercises were physical ones, so I was drawn to a poster I saw hanging outside of our classroom advertising a movement improvisation workshop with Ruth Zaporah, a well-known performance artist. I was captivated by her presence in the videos I watched online and how she blended movement, acting, sound, and improvisation.

After signing up, I learned the workshop was happening in a funky Seattle building that I'd passed many times. Little did I know that within its dilapidated exterior lived a beautiful hall with high ceilings and a glistening wood floor. As light streamed in from an expansive set of windows, I felt immediately drawn to move. People clustered in groups, and, in the middle of one, I spotted a woman with cropped silver-blonde hair and dancing eyes who I guessed was Ruth Zaporah. I was magnetized by her energy; no one I'd ever met had such eyes.

As she performed for us in class, Ruth, at 70-plus, could be wide-eyed and searching one minute, then morose, plaintive, or dull the next. She looked almost feral, like an animal whose life depended on staying alert and rapidly reacting to whatever it noticed. She could morph into a new character with a change of gait or posture and instantly transform a scene.

I want that kind of presence.

Ruth started class by inviting us to walk randomly around the room, following her commands. "Walk. Skip. Freeze. Melt. Lead with your elbows. Walk without making eye contact with anyone, but make sure you don't hit one another." The exercises tuned my sensitivity to my body and to the environment around me. I discovered that if I stayed alert and present, I could come within inches of other people yet never touch them.

Throughout the day, we worked with movement and voice and learned to stay present to the moment. A singing radiator provided the soundtrack for a scene with a partner; a streak of light on the wooden floor became an obstacle to walk or jump across. By the time I left the space at 5 pm, my senses felt tuned in and my imagination turned on. I marveled at the intricacies of light bouncing off a puddle, the music in the whistle of a delivery truck, and the patterns of shapes in the Seattle skyline. I wanted to dance around the passenger deck of the ferry returning me to the island.

Back home, I looked into the mirror and played with my eyes. I opened them wide, squinted them tight, and flashed them back and forth. The woman I saw staring back at me looked animated and alive, silly and sad, enthusiastic and emboldened. From time to time, behind her expressions, I could also see a touch of wild.

Becoming "Pug"

Who knows if I might have enjoyed performing as a child; my nose thwarted my chances of doing so. No leading ladies had noses like mine—"pug noses," as my elementary school companions called them.

Until I was nine years old, it never occurred to me that there was anything unusual about my face. My nose was my nose, and it looked like my dad's—a comparison that made me feel good. But my feelings about my nose changed dramatically in October 1960, when tumble-haired Billy Johnson—who looked like he'd never seen a comb—and crew-cutted Roger Edgars escalated their teasing. Typically, they sat at their little flip-top desks throwing spitballs, pinning gross wads of gum to the undersides of their oak chairs, and passing notes. But when our teacher, Mrs. Richards, dropped her eyes, they turned around and taunted me by playing with my initials. "SF means 'smart fart!' SF means 'smart fart!'"

I tried to ignore them, not wanting to fuel their remarks by acting hurt. *At least they knew I was smart.* But one afternoon, as dark rains descended, they swiveled around in their chairs, pushed their fingers against their nostrils, and snorted. "Pug-nose! Pug-nose!" they shouted. Then they started hysterically giggling and grunting like pigs.

I didn't know what that meant, but I knew it wasn't a compliment.

They've seen something awful, and I'd better figure out what that is. If I can see why they think I'm ugly, they won't be able to hurt me so much.

After a family supper of hot dogs and baked beans, I excused myself, hurried to the upstairs bathroom, flicked on the fluorescent lights over the mirror, and locked the door. I pushed the toothbrushes and glasses out of the way and bent forward until I could see my imperfections in detail.

At first glance, I couldn't see what was so terrible about my nose. I contorted my cheeks and stuck out my lips like a guppy, looking for all traces of ugliness. I pushed and prodded but couldn't find anything *that* awful. Finally, I smashed my fingers against my nostrils and tried snorting. Suddenly it appeared: the dreadful "pig nose," the one they called a "pug."

In that instant, I understood my fate. My face would never fit in. It would never be seen as beautiful or even "regular," and there was nothing I could do about it. (I decided then and there that two short-nosed people should never be allowed to breed.) I knew people would always prefer pretty girls with thin, straight noses. The world thought I was ugly. The sooner I accepted this, the sooner I could get on with my life. No one would be able to surprise me again by calling me defective. I already knew.

Finding the Girl in Madras

Fifty-plus years later, when I was 67, I received an email from my mother's retirement center. It said, "Your mother is no longer entitled to a storage locker now that she has moved from her independent living apartment to assisted living. Please clean out her locker immediately." Apparently, the administrators did not expect their elderly and disabled residents to need space for mementos, photographs, books, luggage, or treasures beyond what could fit in a 300-square-foot room.

My brother, sister, and I convened in the facility's basement to start a two-day cleaning-out marathon. We excavated suitcases, lamps, bins, and a few remaining pieces of Dad's art from her locker. We decided what each of us might want (not much) and made piles to send to the local thrift store. That part of the process was relatively easy.

Going through the snapshots and scrapbooks was not. We set up camp in a bleak, windowless "activities room" to do our sorting, serenaded by the groans of a furnace and the whoosh of a nearby elevator. As we sifted through 20 scrapbooks, 12 photo albums, and 4,712 Kodachrome prints, we kidded each other about how we had looked in our teens. We laughed at my brother's 1960s hair and his curly "king-of-the-jungle" look. We groaned at the image of me taken in 1969, the summer before college, with my permed hair and Indian bedspread dress. We threw photos at each other, including those artificially posed school pictures my mother had faithfully saved.

That's how I ended up with my fourth-grade photograph. In it, I'm wearing a red shirtdress in a madras print that had been in vogue that year. My hair is short-cropped, reminiscent of how I wear it today. My smile is sweet, if cautious. As I stared at my nine-year-old self, goosebumps covered my arms. Something was wrong. This little girl was cute. Maybe even pretty. Definitely appealing.

I couldn't believe she was me.

For 50 years, I had carried around the wound of being called "pug" in third grade. I never wanted to believe that I was ugly, but I tried to accept my fate. Later, as a married woman, I rebuffed my husband's words when he called me "gorgeous," thinking, *He's only saying that because he loves me.* Steve was constantly baffled by my unwillingness to accept his compliments. "How much of that did you take in?" he'd ask whenever he told me I was pretty or even beautiful. "I think you only took in 65 percent of what I said." He was wrong. I bet I took in less than 30 percent of what he said.

But this little girl in madras was not at all ugly. In fact, she was adorable.

I brought the 4x6" photo home and placed it in the corner of our living room, like an altarpiece. I could stare at it when I needed to remember that some stories I carried about myself just weren't true.

Drawing Out Beauty

*As we create beauty, we find the beauty
that lives in us as well.*
—MARCO

I wanted to tell that little girl in madras how beautiful she was with her high cheekbones, smooth forehead, slight smile, and dancing eyes. Even her nose, the one about which she had felt such shame, was interesting. I thought she looked like someone an artist would love to sketch, and I wished I had the skills to do so.

Drawing intrigued me, and books like *Drawing on the Right Side of the Brain* suggested that it was a craft one could learn. When I was 68, I spent a leisurely afternoon in my cabin sorting through my creativity books when one jumped out at me: *Drawing as a Sacred Activity,* by Heather Williams. Flipping through it, I thought, *If I approached the craft as a spiritual activity, maybe I wouldn't worry about whether I had talent. Maybe it would even be fun.*

I checked out Heather's website, discovered that she taught online, and registered for a class she claimed was for everyone—even beginners. I hoped that included confirmed non-drawers like me.

I had always assumed that "real" artists were born knowing how to draw and carried vast mental reservoirs of visual images they could tap into as needed. How else were my artistic friends in grade school able to sit in class and produce images that looked so realistic? It never occurred to me that you had to learn to notice to be able to draw. Having a headful of concepts about horses, birds, and people's faces could never replace careful observation.

During our first session, Heather assured participants that class wasn't about producing beautiful work or getting into art school. She invited us to work with what our eyes noticed rather than what our minds thought we saw. Drawing, using her approach, became a meditation, a way of quieting my mind as I sketched everyday objects like windows, furniture, and doors.

Thirty minutes of close study, pencil in hand, could bring wonder to the ordinary. When I drew my dining room chair, I noticed its curved legs, the pattern on its seat back, and the way it reflected light. After sketching, I never saw it the same way again.

Soon, I was drawing faces. People had always fascinated me, and drawing gave me an excuse to observe them in more detail. On my all-too-frequent video conference calls, I'd whip out a little sketch pad and try to capture the personality of one of the faces I saw on the screen. My "models" didn't know I was drawing them in the few minutes we were together. Every face I drew intrigued me, and I found every one of them attractive.

Heather asked us to create a rough self-portrait. I used one of my press photos and the picture of the girl in madras to guide my drawing. My self-judgments disappeared as I focused on lines and angles and struggled to put the eyes in the right place. My face intrigued and challenged me with its highlights, shadows, and wrinkles. I sketched my high cheekbones and tried to show the twinkle in my eyes.

Sketching noses proved challenging, and mine was no exception. I learned that noses are not little triangles placed in the middle of a head, as they often were in grade school. To represent a nose's shape, I had to use lines, light, and shadow. Portraying warts, wide nostrils, and nose hairs was a puzzle to be solved. In this process, all noses were amazing—including mine.

Slowly, I realized that if I wanted to appreciate more of the world's beauty, I had to appreciate my own. As I gave myself permission to set my own standards, I discovered beauty in a discarded, rusted roll of chicken wire glistening in the rain and the baked swirls of cow dung in a field. I observed it in stumps, rotting leaves and time-weathered faces. Eventually, I could even find it in my own.

Radiance

*I*t's a shame plastic surgery has turned some older people into aliens with unblemished, cosmetically altered faces. I didn't find these compelling to draw. Instead, I preferred to sketch older faces with wrinkles, bags, and sunken eyes. They were far more interesting, and they seemed to hold so many secrets and stories.

The more I studied aging faces, the more I realized that beauty didn't require physical perfection or fitting into a standard of youth. It shone as an inner essence, a light from within, which I called "radiance." In older women who were content to be themselves, radiance glowed through their wrinkles, giving their faces a patina nicked with time. It was as if increasingly translucent skin allowed more of the soul to shine through. Radiance glowed through imperfect teeth, bulging veins, drooping eyelids, and sagging skin. I even found that it could expand as people approached death.

Toward the end of her life, my voice teacher, Peggy, showed me how radiant and beautiful an older face could be. Her skin carried the residue of too many years in the California sun. Yet, when I sang with her, it was as if her age spots and wrinkles disappeared, and only her light remained.

My mother never thought of herself as beautiful. (No wonder it's hard for me!) When I was growing up, I didn't recognize her beauty because I compared her with my friends' more glamorous mothers. They wore designer outfits, went to elite hair salons, and shopped at high-end department stores. My mother bought her clothes on sale at Macy's. She never dyed her hair but kept it mousey-brown and permed until it went naturally gray. Her makeup routine was powder and one shade of rich burgundy lipstick, Revlon 632.

When Mom turned 80, her straight, fine hair turned a luminous silver. This made her eyes and smile stand out more. By the time she reached 90, her lack of designer attire no longer mattered—if it ever did—because she lived in night clothes and hospital gowns. When I visited, I'd find her in bed, her hair oily and plastered to her skull. Blue veins peeked through her temples where her skin was pulled taut against her scalp. Her eyes would glimmer when she recognized me. She looked radiant.

I photographed her, shooting her gnarled hands with their bulging veins and claw-like fingers. I tried to catch the look in her eyes—the wondering one that made her appear as if she were caught between worlds.

When my mother could no longer communicate, her aides assumed that she'd like some lip color, so they gave her some. The lipstick highlighted the little smile Mom would give to family members when they visited.

After she died, I bought two tubes of Revlon 632. My husband hates lipstick, but sometimes I wear it anyway.

Tending
the Spark

Clowning around

"I see a clown in you," my friend Nicki told me in her husky, theatrical voice.

"Clown?" I asked, thinking of those weird and scary circus creatures. I'd gone to her when I was 64 for advice on developing my physical theater and solo performing skills, but this wasn't what I expected.

She laughed, flashing me an elfin grin as she tossed back her tousled blonde hair. "I don't mean a circus clown. In France, where I studied, clowning is taught as a theater art. The European clown is an actor who knows how to use her vulnerabilities on stage to connect with an audience." My ears perked up. Given my abundant supply of vulnerabilities, clowning sounded like a perfect match. "One of my teachers will be in Seattle next week and is giving a four-day clowning workshop. Why don't you sign up?"

"Don't I need experience?"

"You've done improv. You'll do fine and have fun."

I signed up, but on the first night of class, I noticed that the room was full of actors—many with clowning experience. I hoped my "beginner's mind" would be an asset that could get me through. For the first two nights, my lack of experience wasn't a problem. Our room filled with laughter as we played tag, performed silly wordless sketches, and experimented with sounds and gestures. Some of the experienced actors cracked me up; I was forced to grab my belly to keep it from splitting. But, at the end of the second evening, the instructor gave us our homework: "Bring in a trick to perform tomorrow."

What the hell is a trick? I have no idea.

Seeing my panic, a classmate suggested we work together, and, before class the next night, we practiced a classic clown trick: two actors trying to get into the same vest. When we performed, ours started ripping apart, but I didn't worry—I just kept my eyes glued on my partner. With our vest in tatters, we earned a few laughs.

At the start of class on the fourth evening, we participants assembled on the rickety bleachers of our black-walled performance space and awaited instructions. It was a night for solos, or, as I thought of them, chances to fall on your face. Nicki hadn't warned me that our teacher, like many European-trained clowns, had attended the "break-them-to-make-them" school of clowning, where humiliation was a core part of the pedagogy. Within that community, famous teachers helped students find their vulnerabilities by shaming them in front of others. Our workshop instructor was not mean, but she believed in letting students fail—beginners and professionals alike.

She gave us our assignment: "You'll perform individually according to an order I'll give you. When your time comes, go behind the curtain at the back of the stage, and wait for me to put on a piece of music for you. Then, walk out and convey the music's mood. Your job is to make us laugh. But remember, no joking or talking."

I froze. As participant after participant walked out from behind the curtain, I tried to imagine what I could possibly do. Getting the group to laugh looked miserably difficult, and those who tried too hard bombed unless they could turn their pathetic attempts into part of their acts.

When my turn came, I waited behind the curtain with a racing heart and sweat running down my sides. I pulled on a red nose, the only piece of clown attire we ever wore. As my music began, I drew a deep breath, peeked out from behind the curtain, and walked forward. I started dancing, hoping that my rhythmic movements would save me. I swayed and shimmied, but no one in the audience smiled. Then I began moving more frenetically, gesturing, wiggling, and groaning. I prayed that the instructor would throw me a bone of support, since, obviously, I was not a pro.

She didn't. She sat stone-faced in the bleachers while I kept trying—feeling stupider and stupider by the second. Apart from the one woman offering half a smile, the audience stared at me blankly.

When do I self-eject? Where's the magic button that will get me out of here NOW?

Finally, I heard, "Scene!" and left the stage, tail between my legs, holding back my tears. Not only had I failed, no medics were on site to salvage the shards of my deflated ego. I sat in the bleachers for the rest of the evening, using occasional laughter as a veil to keep fellow participants from seeing me stew in my own horribleness.

A classmate attempted to encourage me by saying, "You're older than my mother, and she would never do anything like this." She meant it as a compliment.

I considered my first clowning class to be a spirit-depleting disaster. And I realized that not all my creative experiments had to be successful for me to learn from them. In this case, I learned what I didn't want. Never again would I enroll in the school of shame. I'd had enough of that already; no additional helpings were needed. My spirit was tender, and I needed any suggestions and criticisms coming my way to be couched in ample doses of appreciation, encouragement, and love. I remembered how my ikebana teacher, Nobuko-san, and my voice teacher, Peggy, knew how to always nurture the spark in their students while encouraging them to grow. I renewed my commitment to seek out only supportive teachers.

The morning after my fiasco, Isabel offered her support:

"My dear, don't be hard on yourself. You are sensitive. Count that as a blessing. It's why you can hear Muses and why we can talk. But criticism is so difficult for you. Can you bless that wound and your tenderness? And add it to the compassion you have for others? I'm sure that when you teach, you will always nurture your students' creative sparks."

Two years after my clowning fiasco, at age 64, I tried again. My new teacher invited us to find and share clown moments from our daily lives. That I could do. I performed the making of a fruit smoothie. When I lifted the lid of the blender to check how things were going . . . whoopsie! It took only one second to send yogurt, blueberries, and orange juice flying across the room and one hour to clean it all off the cabinets. My inner stupid came shining through that day, and it gave me—and my classmates—something we could laugh about in class.

Who Gets to Be Called a Writer?

The smell and shape of words surround us.
Words give shape to life.
—MARCO

Without the obligation to teach, I wrote almost every day. Tucked into my big blue recliner chair in my cabin, I enjoyed playing with words, phrases, and ideas through my blogs and the short pieces I shared with a writing class. But I didn't call myself a "real writer."

With clowning, I didn't worry about being "a real clown," and with improv, I didn't worry about being "a real improviser." Whatever I did was fine, as long as I felt like I was learning and enjoying myself. But writing felt more serious. Real writers, I had decided, grew up with journals tucked under their pillows in grade school. They composed poems by flashlight, published their first novels in high school, and attended journalism or fine arts programs. I was not one of them.

Still, I was intrigued by the craft and wanted to improve my skills. When a friend raved about a six-day workshop called "The Self as the Source of the Story" with Northwest writer Christina Baldwin, I signed up. The time and tuition required felt like a commitment to my writing life.

We met on Whidbey Island in Puget Sound, at an older retreat site nestled into the edges of a large marsh. On the first afternoon of the workshop, I walked down a squishy alder-lined path to reach the large yurt that housed our classes. I enjoyed the sight of a hawk, the sound of a chorus of crows, and the smell of sweet red cedar. The late afternoon sun glowed through the windows as Christina convened the circle of 15 and invited each of us to introduce ourselves. Some participants were published authors, while others, like me, were just plunging into the craft. No matter. Christina welcomed us all as she outlined the week's plan: three-and-a-half days of class exercises and discussions, followed by a day and a half in silence, writing on our own. On the last morning, we'd read the fruits of our work.

When we convened on day two, Christina asked us, "What do you each plan to work on during your silent day?"

I balked as the previous day's excitement turned into dread. *No fair! I'm not prepared to answer. I don't know what I'll do because I'm not working on anything.*

Christina used a beautifully carved Northwest native plank as the "talking stick" in our circle. As members took the stick, they described the memoirs, essays, and fiction pieces which they planned to work on. My mind raced ahead as I saw the stick approaching. Nothing about my life seemed important enough to write about. After all, who was I? Just a woman living on an island, trying to invent a more creative life after 50. Not a celebrity. Not someone who had made millions of dollars, endured horrific trauma, or survived a spellbinding adventure. I was ordinary. My gremlins chimed in: *"Your story doesn't matter."*

Then, my neighbor to the right passed me the stick. Before speaking, I brushed away a few tears and used the edge of my gray sweatshirt to wipe my nose. The woman to my left slipped me a tissue as I said:

"I want to write about my journey after midlife. But who cares? Maybe I'd have a story if I were famous and could say, 'I used to be a high-profile executive in New York City and traveled the world. But then, I gave it up to move to a 200-acre farm in upstate New

York, where I fell in love with country living. Now, my goat herds have won regional prizes and been featured in The New York Times Magazine. *Chefs from New York City drive to the farm just to stock up on my cheeses. And a publisher approached me last week with a book deal. Now that would be a story."*

My classmates laughed, since many of them were harboring similar doubts. Why would anyone care to read our stories? Who would even notice what we had to say?

Christina responded gently to a question she had heard at least a thousand times. "You write because it is *your* story. You have a story to share, and that's the story you need to tell."

I blew my nose and nodded.

OK. I will trust and write.

During the silent day, I worked from breakfast through dusk. On a break to clear my head, I walked the paths through the marsh, admiring the grasses and the lichen coating many of the trees. An eagle soared above looking for its next salmon dinner. I would have liked to wander more, even in the cold drizzle, but I had editing to do. I revised late into the evening and woke early to complete my piece minutes before we reconvened. After a few classmates had shared their work, I read several pages of mine and relished the smiles and appreciation that followed. Then, Christina offered strong words of encouragement. Leaving the retreat, I knew I had shifted; for the first time, I could call myself "a writer."

When I resumed my life at home, the label didn't matter. What mattered was that I keep writing—and I did.

The Writing Life

Beware what you choose to create,
because it can begin to create you.
—SJF, AGE 67

The artist belongs to his work,
not the work to the artist.
—Novalis

The idea of writing a book had never crossed my radar. After I returned from Christina's workshop, I wrote essays, poems, and weekly blogs. I worked on stories that I hoped to perform. I improved my website and made my words sound more natural. I helped others to craft their stories.

Isabel and I had been talking almost daily for a couple of years when she announced, *"It's time to write a book about your journey with creativity and aging—people need your story."*

With all she had given me, I didn't want to be disrespectful to Isabel, but I wondered if she, living in Muse-land, had any idea how much I was carrying. *"Great idea—remind me next year."* I was up to my elbows in revising my website, coaching clients, and doing occasional teaching. I told her, *"Maybe I'll think about it after I get my new business direction off the ground."*

Isabel knew not to push, but one week later, she was at it again in her gentle, persuasive way. *"I think the book is important to your path, my dear. Why don't you see where it will go?"*

I kept rebuffing, but on her third try (week four), I knew I'd been licked. *OK. Maybe I can write a book in a year while I continue to work. It could be a self-help book based on my clients' experiences, a few best creative practices, and a review of books on aging.*

She was smart enough to not tell me what I was really in for.

"Good," she said, *"just remember to love the process."*

I began jotting down ideas and reading works on creativity and aging. I played with outlines and toyed with different structures. I delighted in words and explored different narratorial voices. I interviewed other people with relevant stories. Occasionally, I tore my hair out, and I hired a coach for some extra support. Then, as my efforts gained momentum, the book began taking over. It became my point of focus, and my client work dwindled. But by then, I was hooked.

Isabel had not warned me about how demanding a book could become. Three years into the writing process, it started bossing me around, telling me to move away from the self-help genre and any pretense of being an enlightened "thought leader" who told others what to do. The book insisted that I focus on my story and write from my experience—with humility.

"Beware what you choose to create," I would later write, "because it can begin to create you."

I initially pushed back against the book's direction, as I had with Isabel. *"You're asking me to write what sounds like a memoir. Sharing my personal story like that is not in the plan. After all, I have a PhD, which gives me the right to be an authority who can share her expertise with others."*

Isabel reminded me, *"Is that really what you want, my dear? Haven't you been working to lose that old academic voice and write more naturally like you do in your blog?"*

When I gathered a few friends for a first reading of introductory chapters, they confirmed Isabel's perspective. One even told me, "This is interesting, but I like your blog voice better. It's so much more personal."

So much for being a "thought leader."

As I surrendered to the guidance and shifted to a more personal story, the work came alive, even though I was no longer sure which way to go.

"You don't have to know. Just take the next step," Isabel reminded— good counsel for the book and my life. On the days when I sank into a pit of self-doubt, she suggested rereading what I had written about trusting the call I had heard.

"Trust the book, my dear, and let it lead you forward."

The book was becoming a guide, one that would teach me much about discipline, perseverance, and, ultimately, love.

But I'm getting ahead of myself because, as I wrote the book, another great teacher stepped up to help me, one who had been with me since my forties: Death.

Death, My Assigned Teacher

"Get up, Brio"

"Get up, Brio! Get up!!!" I screamed at the body that lay crumpled on the ground. "Enough of your antics. Get up and let me groom you."

"He can't, Sally," the horsewoman standing by me said. "He's dead."

I shivered as the air temperature dropped. Just five minutes earlier, it had been a beautiful, cloudless June day—perfect weather for a trail ride on my beautiful chestnut gelding. He, however, would have preferred to stay in the field with the herd instead of working with me. It had taken some effort to tie him to my horse trailer so I could groom him, tack him up, and prepare to ride. He had snorted and jigged in place, threatening to break the bungee cord that stretched between his halter and the trailer, keeping him tied. At one point, he began pulling back so fiercely that I thought he might topple the trailer. Instead, he took a step to the side and the bungee went slack. Without the tension on the cord, he jerked his head and hit it on the trailer.

In that instant, he collapsed and fell to the ground as I watched, immobilized.

This can't be real.

My voice disappeared—I couldn't talk or sob—but internally, I pleaded. *God, please, rewind the last 30 seconds. Just 30 seconds is all that I want—so that my horse can be alive and fiery again. Don't let this be real.*

But Death was very real and not interested in bargaining. I wasn't prepared to face this force that was to become my teacher, even though I'd had made its acquaintance when I lost my grandparents, a few pets, and my first horse. I'd grown up believing that I always had some control over what happened to me. Death shattered that illusion.

I can't bear this. It was bad enough when my first horse, Gaelen, was shot by a drug-addled teenager two years ago. That was horrendous, but I survived. I constructed a story with a silver lining—that Gaelen's death allowed me to buy Brio, a gorgeous, talented, and younger horse. But now that tale's been smashed, and Brio's dead on the ground. This time, there's no silver lining to ease the pain.

The summer of Gaelen's death, in my 46th year, I passed through clouds of numbness and showers of grief. When I found Brio, the skies opened up, and the joy of riding helped me forget the pain of loss. But Brio's loss brought it back and added more.

Death had entered my life as my new teacher, formidable, demanding and wise. I didn't know how soon the next lesson would be coming.

Death Training

My father was diagnosed with non-Hodgkin's lymphoma one year after Brio died.

My experience with death thus far between friends and horses had taught me:

~ Surrendering to grief often leads to compassion for others.

~ Death could come anytime; it's an illusion to think that it won't.

~ By letting sorrow slow me down and break my heart, I could experience beauty in art, music, and nature with new depth.

But as Dad began his two-year struggle with cancer, my death training was about to accelerate. I devoured books by doctors, caretakers, and patients close to death. I deluged hospice workers with questions like: "How will I know when Dad is near the end?" "What might his dying look like?" and "How can I best help someone who is about to pass?" I was still frightened by the idea of death, and I wanted to know what I—and everyone around me—would be facing.

Dad started chemotherapy, and his cancer went into remission nine months later. Our family was ecstatic—until the disease returned in three months and never left again. At the start of his second year of cancer, I traveled two hours north to the Whidbey Institute on Whidbey Island to attend a seminar with end-of-life experts. Sitting in front of a roaring fireplace in the Institute's great hall, I listened as speakers described the dying process.

After reading so much about death, I thought I knew what a "good" or "spiritual" death looked like. In my idyllic image, family and friends come together to bless and support the person who is passing. All old wounds have been forgiven, and all necessary conversations have happened. The family sits at the bedside of the departing one, reading prayers and listening to their loved one's last reflections. Soft music plays—possibly on a harp. Near the moment of departure, everyone professes their love while holding the hands of their beloved as they pass.

The presenters of the workshop shot my vision down. There was no "good death," they said, no gold standard in dying to achieve. They explained that the process of dying took on a wide variety of guises, and we needed to allow its mystery to unfold. Forgiveness was still a good idea, as was listening to and honoring the wishes of the departing one. Love was always welcome, and profound conversations were great. But, if someone died alone without soft music playing, that didn't make theirs a "bad death."

They advised us to learn as much as we could about the process of dying rather than work to make death fit our preconceptions. The end-of-life experts recommended that we spend time with the dying and learn what it was like to be present and open to their experiences. We should try to respond with care and curiosity to whatever arose at the end, even if we couldn't understand it. This workshop helped me to form my own vision for supporting a loved one through this process:

Being with a friend nearing the end of life is like the ultimate improv. We listen as our partner, the dying person, makes a move or says a word. Then we "say yes" by acknowledging whatever our partner has offered and responding. In so doing, we both advance into the unknown.

I was glad to have let go of my ideas about "a good death" when it was Dad's time to pass. He wanted to die at home, and our family arranged his care to make that possible. During his two years with cancer, I felt so grateful to be with him, knowing how much he had always loved me. Any past issues looked trivial compared to the love I felt in the present.

I spent hours sobbing on my meditation room floor, praying for Dad and feeling held by my Longing—hours which became like a time of communion. As his death approached, my contemplations deepened. I felt like my heart was being emptied and filled with a new kind of knowing. I asked, *"What really matters?"* and heard, once again, *"There's more."* I knew that there was *more* to life, including an energy or life force beyond what I could see. I often called it God—a word that worked for me. Yet, even that word failed to describe the sense of Presence and Mystery I felt as Dad neared the end.

On November 25th, 1999, the family celebrated our last Thanksgiving Day with him, knowing he was close to departing. Despite all the media buzz about the new millennium, Dad showed no interest in experiencing it. What he wanted instead was to live until December 3rd so that he could celebrate his 50th anniversary with Mom—a gift he knew mattered the world to her. My sister, brother, and I planned a party for that date in their honor, but by December 1st, Dad was failing. It was nip and tuck whether he would make it to the big day. On the afternoon of the 3rd, I gave him the card and small pendant he had asked me to buy for Mom. With a shaking hand he scrawled a message: "Honey, we did it. Love, David."

I drove him to the anniversary party at my sister's, and he managed to stay for two hours, holding court on the couch and accepting congratulations from a host of friends. Then, exhausted, he asked my husband to take him home while Mom stayed and enjoyed the company. The next morning, he began hospice care and his final week.

During his last days, our family made sure that one of us was always with him. For most of that week, he seemed peaceful. He smiled and received our love. I sat with him and stared at the photos on the wall behind his bed. There, I saw Dad as a toddler in Victorian-style bloomers and as a twentysomething in his lieutenant's cap during WWII. I saw the family man posed next to a fireplace for the yearly posed Christmas shot with his family, and I saw the corporate guy looking gray and weary. In one photo, a grinning Dad held his granddaughter on his knees. Staring at the photo wall, I realized that the dad lying before me still carried all of his many ages within him.

Why do we spend so much money and effort trying to be young when we always carry our youth within us?

Two days before his end, he increased his morphine drips to deal with the pain. Suddenly, his behavior changed. He would bolt upright in bed, with eyes bulging and face contorted into an "O" as if he were screaming. He reminded me of the terrified man pictured in Edvard Munch's painting "The Scream." During a dozen such episodes, family members watched him, unsure where he had gone. Was he seeing a memory from WWII or reliving an emotional wound? We would never know.

I tried to calm him by chanting at his bedside: "I love you. I love you. I love you." He would look out at me and, for a moment, his eyes would soften, and he would relax and stop his inward scream. Finally, at the end of that long day (helped, perhaps, by additional morphine), he was able to relax and sleep.

I stayed in his room that night, lying on a twin bed near him, holding watch so that my mother could sleep. As the gaps between his inhalations and exhalations increased, I counted the seconds, wondering *Was that it? Did Death just take him?* At 2 am, my world became singularly focused on the seconds between each breath, and, of course, the love. I sank into a space of gratitude, almost without emotion, where I hung on to each precious second of beingness still left to us.

My father died at 4 pm, December 12, 1999, during the first moment in three days that he'd been alone. We'd all taken a break and left his side because he looked so peaceful.

I walked into the bedroom, discovered his dead body, and said good-bye. I told the others he was gone, and we cried. My heart gaped open, yet I felt graced to have been with him on his last night.

I continued to cry as I sat in the living room waiting for his body to be taken away. But I had no regrets about his death. Dad had left us in his way, and it was perfectly fine.

"The Surgery is Supposed to Be Over"

As Steve moved into his seventies, he developed heart problems that required high-tech surgical procedures called "catheter ablations." These attempts to cure his atrial fibrillation required cauterizing the places where his heart was misfiring. Before each operation, Steve's surgeon would reassure us that the procedure was safe while also telling us that an errant cut could permanently damage his lungs. Before his fifth procedure, the doctor said, "I think I can safely go deeper this time and get the last of the misfires." The idea—and the phrase "I think"—made me nervous, but Steve trusted the doctor and gave him the go-ahead.

The four-hour surgery was scheduled for noon on a Wednesday. I was glad that I had my weekly ikebana class that day, as it would provide me with two hours of sanctuary while I awaited the hospital's call.

When the day of the surgery arrived, I measured my life in minutes:

1:50 pm. I arrived at class early and sat in the darkened space before others came, enjoying the creative vibe I felt among the construction papers, shiny beads, popsicle sticks, tempera paints, pencils, scissors, baskets, and brushes. The air carried the faint odors of glue and borax.

2 pm. My classmates entered, along with Nobuko-san, who passed out floral materials and gave us individualized instructions. I let fellow participants know what was happening with Steve, and they offered their empathy; they knew what it was like to wait for a hospital call. Then, I

set to work on an arrangement of chrysanthemum blossoms and large, shiny, fatsia leaves.

3 pm. I finished my piece and asked Nobuko-san to offer her thoughts. She turned the low, flat container a few degrees counterclockwise, walked around it, and said, "Very good." Then she added one more flower. I thanked her and glanced at the clock. It might be another hour before I heard about Steve. I asked Nobuko-san, "Could I make another arrangement?" She nodded and handed me three roses and some pine branches.

Focus on your work. Don't think about Steve. He's fine.

4 pm. I finished my second arrangement. Nobuko-san approved, and I packed up my stuff. Class was over, but I still had no news.

Don't think about it.

"Domo arigato gozimasu," I said to Nobuko-san, with the hint of a bow. I left the room and walked to a nearby arboretum. Only a few trees kept their fall leaves, but a collection of witch hazel dazzled me with its orange and scarlet winter blooms.

Focus on Beauty. Steve has had this procedure before; it isn't open-heart surgery.

5 pm. Still no word. I headed to the hospital. When I got to the room where Steve would be living for the next two days, the nurses invited me to sit and wait there.

6:30 pm. I looked at the clock. The surgery was now running two hours late, and I still had no word from the doctor. The Seattle skies had turned dark. A chorus of questions flooded my mind as I stared blankly at the city lights.

What would life be without Steve? How much longer will we be together? How much longer can we stay on our land? Could I manage the property without him?

I thought of the simple things we did together: Eat popcorn. Watch silly movies. Clean moths out of the pantry. Chop down blackberries. Pick raspberries.

Chores are fun when they're done together. I don't want to do them alone.

7 pm. I remembered the fights from our early days. He forgot to buy an onion. I didn't close a cabinet door. Now, 25 years into our marriage, arguments rarely happened.

What would I do without him?

Steve fixed the car, paid bills, mowed the property, and anchored me through life. I almost took him for granted, except that I didn't. I stared at the clock.

How much time did we have? How many more Christmases? Sunsets?

7:15 pm. His doctor walked in, tired but full of good news. "Everything went fine. I had to do a little more than expected, but I think we got it all this time. Steve will be back in the room soon."

Just as he finished speaking, an aide rolled Steve in. His face beamed as he caught sight of me—a look I'll never forget.

I wished I could erase the previous hours' doubts and put my fears back into the box from which they'd sprung. But it was too late. I had already counted the Christmases. If we were lucky, we might have 20.

Walking in Beauty

I watched in awe as Jaralene assembled a garden feast on our dining room table. She placed radishes carefully cut into roses, jicama julienned into slices, and multi-colored baby carrots onto a hand-painted floral platter. Then she mixed a vinaigrette to accompany a salad of fresh-picked arugula and lettuce. She brought out a dilled potato salad, bread she had baked, and a cobbler with last year's blueberries. Lunch was her way of thanking the volunteers who would be assisting at my property during the 2011 Vashon Garden Tour. And she had a way of making everything she did so artful.

I was blessed that Jaralene had offered to be my "garden angel" for the tour, overseeing the movements of workers and guests around the property. With her characteristic ease, she calmed my last-minute nerves and ensured that everything on the day of the event flowed seamlessly.

She called later that summer to tell me she'd received a diagnosis of pancreatic cancer. News of that disease is never good, but I prayed that she'd beat it with her generous spirit and positivity. Wanting to channel my sadness into help, I organized a dozen friends to put Jaralene's extensive English-style country garden to bed before winter. On a blustery day that fall, we convened to weed, prune, laugh, rake, and send loving thoughts to our friend. At one moment during the afternoon, she appeared on her porch above the garden. Standing in a fleece jacket with a chemo cap covering her bald head, she smiled at us and waved, as if offering a blessing.

Following our weed-a-thon, I wrote a poem for Jaralene—or "almost a poem," since, at that time, I thought poetry was a sophisticated craft I had not yet mastered. Nevertheless, words spilled out of me:

We cut stalks of asters, bee balm, hostas
Pull sweet peas long gone
Divide sage and iris
Thin rugosas
Nourish soil with dark compost
to soften the attack of winter rains.

Knowing the chemo
will pummel your body
in order to protect it,
we prune hebes, roses, lavender,
tuck red tulips and golden daffodils
into cold soil.
Dream of the day in spring,
quince and currents blossoming,
we return to your garden,
to celebrate life.
And you will be whole.

Jaralene loved the poem, and I felt grateful to have been able to use writing as a channel for my hope and grief.

She pursued chemotherapy and other remedies for five years, but her cancer never quit. I didn't see her often, but when I did, our conversations ran deep. Jaralene could talk about the challenges of chemo one moment and the delights of seeing her grandchildren the next. She never lost her enthusiasm for life.

After her chemo stopped working, Jaralene invited me to have tea with her on her porch. She placed two floral china cups on a tray and carried them outside while I greeted her husband, Tom. As Jaralene and I drank our tea, we talked about the workshop she had recently attended based on John O'Donohue's book *Beauty*. We discovered how much his work spoke to us both.

Directly below her porch sat her summer garden, with colors that could have been painted by an impressionist. The delphiniums' deep blue complemented the indigo of her ripening blueberries. Orange day lilies danced in the sun, celebrating their brief lives. Pink and white climbing roses sent sweetness into the air. Jaralene led me down the garden's paths, pointing out her favorite flowers before returning toward the house. I gave her my hand as we walked up the steep stone stairs leading to her porch. "Jaralene," I said, "I love your garden, but it must be a lot of work for you and Tom to maintain."

She sighed and nodded. "Yes. I wonder if Tom will be able to handle it when I'm gone."

I gulped. Although she and I had talked about death, we'd never acknowledged how near she was to her end. *Would she want to talk more?*

"Have you thought about what you'd like for your memorial?" I asked cautiously, watching her face to see if I had gone too far.

Without missing a beat, she said, "No, but maybe it's time."

I took a deep breath. "I'll take notes if you want to talk through your ideas."

We moved to her kitchen table, and Tom soon joined us. Her voice became animated as she described what she wanted: friends, fresh raspberries, poetry, a few short talks, and a buffet of local foods. "Could we give the guests bags of my purple poppy seeds?" she asked. Tom nodded.

As I was leaving, Jaralene and Tom thanked me for opening this conversation. I thanked them in return, knowing I had received a gift:

sacred time to anchor myself in what mattered. I drove home thinking about Steve, my mother, and the flowers in the garden—all of which I loved yet could not hold on to.

When I returned to my house, I roamed through our garden and picked out a set of camellia branches and dahlia blossoms. I bent the branches slowly, then placed them into an arrangement with the flowers, my heart heavy. The beauty of the flowers comforted me as I thought of losing her and, someday, losing Steve.

Later that afternoon, I took out my copy of John O'Donohue's *Beauty* and turned to a quote I'd marked:

> *"The human soul is hungry for beauty; we seek it everywhere in landscape, music, art, clothes, furniture, gardening, companion-ship, love, religion, and in ourselves . . . When we experience the Beautiful, there is a sense of homecoming."*

Jaralene's memorial took place the following spring. It was her last work of art.

Stay or Go

In 2018, I read Steven Cope's book, *The Great Work of Your Life,* about using the ancient Hindu text, *The Bhagavad Gita,* to make critical life decisions. Little did I know how relevant it was about to become to me.

I'd read it in anticipation of flying to India for a conference called "The Bhagavad Gita and Leadership." Mom had just turned 90, and, given her health, I rarely traveled. But the invitation had been too tempting—especially when an Indian corporation offered to cover my airfare in exchange for two days of teaching. I talked with my siblings, and we agreed that I should go. Despite our concerns about Mom, we needed to live our lives. We could cover for each other in Seattle.

When I arrived at an ashram in Pune, India, for the event, I was exhausted. But the sound of morning temple bells and the vistas of pastel hills gently revived me. For the next four days, I attended presentations, meditations, and art, music, and dance events in the large lecture hall. The backdrop was always a 15-foot-high brilliant orange and red banner that depicted a scene from the *Gita.* I was captivated by the image of the tall, handsome warrior prince, Arjuna, driving four charging white steeds with the god Shiva at his side. I knew from Cope's book that Arjuna had struggled deeply with life's questions, including how to divide his service among the competing concerns of war, work, community, and family.

When the conference ended, I headed to Mumbai to teach for the firm that had underwritten my airfare. After months of prepping,

I couldn't wait to present my work on "leadership storytelling." I stayed at the company's guest apartment, where, on the morning of my first class, the cook served me a simple breakfast of rice, toast, tea, and yogurt. As I waited for the company chauffeur to pick me up and transport me through Mumbai's intense snarled traffic, I took a moment to check my phone. A text from my sister popped up: "Mom had a major stroke. Unless you object, she's going into hospice care."

Despite the time zone differences between Mumbai and Seattle, I called my sister right away. I learned that Mom was in bed, partially paralyzed and barely able to speak. No one knew how long she might live. My head swirled with questions: *Should I leave? Should I stay? What was my duty to the client, to Mom, and to myself?*

I thought of Arjuna. Even if I abandoned my work and caught a flight out of India that evening, I had no guarantee of reaching Mom in time. So, I prayed. Prayer had increasingly become part of my life, though my version of it stuck to its simplest forms. Some of my prayers were a mere *"Thank you"* or *"I know you're there—at least, I hope you are."* Other times, they were an SOS to whatever benevolent guardian spirit might be listening—Christ, Mary, Tara, God, Shiva, Buddha, or an ancestor. *"If you're out there, please help."*

In Mumbai I asked, *"What should I do?"* An answer came through immediately:

~ Complete my work assignment.

~ Teach with an open heart.

~ Trust that I would see my mother again.

During my workshops, I talked about Arjuna, and my students offered their prayers for my mother. I flew home right after finishing my teaching, and Steve picked me up at the airport. "She's still alive," he told me as we drove across Seattle, "but she can't communicate much." An hour later, I was sitting next to her, babbling again and again, "I love you. I love you. I love you." Mom couldn't speak a complete sentence, but she didn't need to. Seeing her mouth try to form "I love you" was enough.

The Long Wait

When our hearts are wintry, grieving, or in pain,
Yet Thy touch can call us back to life again.
FROM THE HYMN "NOW THE GREEN BLADE RISETH"

I would repeat those three words—"I love you"—as Mom lay in bed for the next two and a half years. The same mother who once told me, "I never want to be dependent or confined to bed," appeared to be in no hurry to die. Resting on a pulsing mattress that kept her body free from bed sores, she seemed content to lie there indefinitely. Every day, she ate her slurry mush and drank whatever her aides offered her.

I couldn't fathom why she was choosing to live. Maybe her soul had decided that after a lifetime of caring for everyone else, she deserved time to reflect and receive care from others. Whatever the reason, waiting for her to die became an emotional boot camp and an opportunity to face what I could not control—something that has never been easy for me. Emotions whipped through me like mini-tornados on a daily basis. They ranged from poignant sadness to fiery frustration and anger. Sometimes, I felt kind and giving; other times, I felt selfish and greedy. I worried that Mom would run through her money and need support from her family if she lived more than a few years longer. Then, I felt petty for those thoughts. I coached myself, saying:

It's her money. Having her with us is more valuable than any inheritance. Every moment with her is precious. She gets to choose how long she lives.

My self-coaching helped some, but mostly, I learned to tolerate what I could not change.

In her last months, Mom stopped talking altogether and slept through most of her days. I sat at her bedside listening to the inhalation and exhalation of her mattress pump and studying her face. I touched her skin, caressed the baby-smooth surfaces of her face, and massaged her bony shoulders. The mother who had once carried me was so reduced that I could almost carry her. Yet, she remained as radiant as she had been when I first started sketching her. It was as if the nearing presence of Death had given her a glow.

Occasionally, I slipped three of my fingers into the clasp formed by her bony fingers and palm, and felt her gripping me, like a bird clasping its perch.

When we could no longer have conversations, I sang to her. Although I was reluctant to sing in public, I figured Mom was a captive audience, especially with her door shut. I improvised songs: "Once upon a time, there was a family in New Canaan . . . ," I riffed. "You were the best Mom, and we are so grateful." What I said or how I sounded hardly mattered. Even the slightest smile on her face was a reward I treasured.

Hoping to comfort her, I sang about God, going home, and hopes for the afterlife, all topics over which I had absolutely no authority. "*Your mother and your father are waiting to welcome you Home,*" I chanted, crossing my fingers that it might be true.

On the last day I visited, I brought Mom a bouquet of peonies, straight from the garden, but she didn't open her eyes. Sitting lightly on her bed, I wondered why she was unwilling to look at me. At a loss for what to do, I found a few Christian hymns on the internet that didn't sound preachy or punishing, such as, "Now the Green Blade Riseth." With a melody that dates to the 15th century and haunting lyrics, it was one of my favorites.

"Now the green blade riseth, from the buried grain
Wheat that in the dark earth many days has lain.
Love lives again, that with the dead has been:
Love is come again, like wheat that springeth green . . ."

I began the next verse, singing,
"When our hearts are wintry, grieving, or in pain."

Then my voice cracked. I was singing about myself. *My* heart was wintry; *I* was grieving. I wanted God to be there for us both.

"Yet Thy touch can call us back to life again,
Fields of our hearts that dead and bare have been:
Love has come again like wheat that springeth green."

I sensed in that moment that the room had stilled. The air felt potent and thin, as if we were standing close to the veil that separated life from death. The Celts, I later learned, talk about "thin places" as spots where the heavens are nearest the Earth. I felt that Mom and I had entered a sacred bubble where time had stopped and being together was all that there was.

I began to sing "How Great Thou Art," a favorite hymn we had both sung in church:

"Oh Lord, my God
When I, in awesome wonder
Consider all the worlds Thy hands have made

I see the stars, I hear the rolling thunder
Thy power throughout the universe displayed.
Then sings my soul, my Savior God, to Thee
How great Thou art, how great Thou art."

When I got to the chorus, I heard a deep sigh coming from the bed. It was the first sound Mom had made since I arrived. Her eyelids fluttered.

You heard me, Mom. You were listening.

I kept singing.

"Then sings my soul, my Savior God to Thee
How great Thou art, how great Thou art."

I left, not knowing whether I would see her alive again.

My cell phone rang the following Wednesday morning while I was at Zumba class. When I was done dancing, I checked the message. It read: "Your mother died at 9:40 am."

I keened. A voice I didn't recognize rose from my gut—a wail that shook the dressing room walls and spread through the dance studio. My dance mates stopped their conversations and ran to embrace me. I said, "My mother is gone."

The long wait was over.

The Foster Dog

When Mom began to decline in her late eighties, even before she experienced the stroke that left her bedridden, I wondered how I would deal with her loss. An inspiration popped into my head: *I'll get another springer spaniel.*

Steve and I had stayed dogless for 15 years after our previous springer, Lady, died. Lady had been a faithful companion, seeing me through the rough spots in my early teaching career. The morning after she passed, I could barely function. But living without a dog had made life less complicated. When we traveled, our elderly cat, Barry, required minimal care, and we agreed that he deserved to live his final years dog-free.

I was 65 when Mom had her stroke. By the time she passed two and a half years later, I had forgotten my vision of getting a dog. On a whim, six months before her death, I decided to do a little "dog therapy" by volunteering online for English Springer Rescue America (ESRA). Screening potential adoption families gave me a reason to gorge on pictures of my favorite breed.

Then, one week after Mom's memorial, in July 2018, I received an SOS from ESRA's regional director. The Seattle Animal Shelter had called her to say they had picked up an emaciated springer that was spending his time at their facility shaking and cowering. The staff liked him and had named him Riley. They thought he was partially deaf, blind, and possibly demented. The ESRA director wanted to get him into foster care immediately. Her email message read: "We need to get Riley from the shelter today. Can you help foster?"

Tears welled as I thought about this frightened little springer. I went to Steve and described the situation. "Darling, I know this is sudden, but could we consider fostering Riley?"

With his steady wisdom, Steve replied, "Honey, be sensible. Barry deserves to live out his last days peacefully. Think of how upset he would be."

"I know." My love of springers had clouded my good sense. I emailed the director, saying, "Sorry, no." Then I tried to put Riley out of mind, trusting he would find a good home.

The following morning, I emailed her again to assure myself that Riley was OK. She wrote back immediately. "One of our best foster families took him out of the shelter yesterday, but he's fighting with their dogs. We have to find him a new home today."

My heart flooded with a force that suggested that my Longing was sending me a message.

OMG. Why did I check back with the director? We can't take in Riley. So, why do I keep sobbing?

I went to Steve, barely able to speak. "Honey, I know you're not happy about the idea of fostering Riley, so you don't have to say 'yes.' But I need to know . . . are you saying an absolute 'no' to fostering?"

Ten minutes later, Steve had readied our van for an emergency doggy pick-up. (You see why I love my husband so much!) We agreed to rendezvous with Riley's first foster family at a Seattle park near the ferry. Before we left, we installed a wooden baby gate to divide the house into dog and cat zones.

As we approached the park, I caught sight of a little brown-and-white dog walking in circles on a leash. It had to be Riley. The foster family, veterans of many springer rescues, gifted us with an old doggy bed, biscuits, and a pound of food, which we gratefully accepted, since we were completely unprepared. Then Steve carefully lifted the relentlessly panting Riley into our van. Five minutes later, as we sat in the ferry line, Steve turned to me and said, "I'm really glad we're doing this." We had both fallen under the spell of this needy pooch.

Barry adapted to the new arrangement as we showered love on our new family member. We fed Riley, walked him, and took him to the vet for extensive dental surgery. We spent hours sitting with him on the floor, caressing and cuddling him. He gained a little weight. But nothing we tried, from drugs to telepathic energy healings, stopped his panting.

I suspected Riley had neurological damage, since he couldn't wag his tail. After a few months with us, he began to have problems with incontinence. Four months into our fostering, I left for a conference, and, upon my return, Steve told me that Riley had gotten stuck in the bathroom, wedged between the toilet and the wall. He'd spent a night whimpering and soiling himself. Clearly, his confusion, incontinence, and dementia were increasing.

We called the ESRA director, and the three of us agreed: It was time.

At the vet's, the staff escorted us into a back room reserved for doggy departures. I sat with Riley on the cold cement floor, crying and staring at bottles filled with gauze, alcohol, and biscuits. I rubbed his face. When the vet came in, I asked her between sniffles, "Can Riley have another biscuit?" She nodded.

The vet was gentle, and the room was quiet as she gave the injection. Steve wiped tears off of his glasses. Looking at Riley's stilled body, I felt like my heart had been drop-kicked. It didn't matter that Riley was "just" a foster dog who'd only been with us for four months. Grief roared through me, making it impossible to attend to anything else that day.

I clipped a small stash of hair from Riley's tail, thinking I'd bury it in the woodlands near my cabin, close to Mom's ashes. A friend said,

"Grieving Riley might be your way of grieving your mom." She was right. Mom's departure had taken such a long time and brought up many complex feelings. When she died, I had become almost numb to her loss—even as I would soon discover how much I missed her over the years that followed. My love for Riley, on the other hand, had been simple and uncomplicated. He had been with us for only four months, but he had stolen our hearts. His loss left me raw, with nothing to buffer my tears.

By the time of Riley's death, I had lost three horses, my parents, my friends Lynn and Jaralene, my cousin Brenda, and multiple aunts and uncles. Soon, Barry the cat would leave us as well. With each loss, I learned that Grief, like Death, was a forceful teacher. It would not be controlled, nor would it agree to a schedule outlining how long it would stick around.

Yet, however painful, death and grief were bringing energy to my creative work. They helped make my words more raw, specific, and honest. They asked me to dig deeper within myself and be truthful. They invited me to ask, *"What matters?* and, *"Why do I let the past limit the ways in which I can create?"*

I knew that Death could appear at any moment, and I would sometimes ask myself, *Am I using my days on Earth fully? Or am I spending too much time on things that don't matter?* I was doing both, of course—as we all do. I didn't believe in a Last Judgment, that dire event I learned about in Sunday school. Still, I questioned whether I was fulfilling my purpose—that is, if there was a purpose for living beyond just being here, loving, and learning.

Trying to answer this question intellectually proved futile. My heart was a better guide. When it was open, I could more gracefully hold life's many contradictions. I could want to know my purpose *and* be OK with not being sure. I could fear death *and* accept it.

I knew that the emotions of sorrow and joy did not cancel each other out; one could sweeten the other. The pain of losing friends made me want to spend more time with the ones I had left. And my fear of losing Steve? It was difficult to face; yet, it invited me to savor the quiet moments and simple times we still had together.

Six months after we lost Riley, I picked out a shaded part of the garden where ferns and hostas grew and dug a hole for the bits of his fur I'd clipped at the vet's. When we lost Barry, just months after Riley, we buried him there as well. By feeding the Earth and new life, I worked with my grief.

A few weeks later, I received another call from ESRA inviting us to foster-to-adopt two young and healthy springer spaniel brothers. We could try them out, the ESRA director said, then decide whether we wanted to adopt. The only caveat: They came as a pair. We immediately said yes. Winston and Royce came bounding into our lives full-tilt, creating chaos with their four-year-old intensity. I hadn't anticipated the work it would take to continually sweep dirt, mud, and hair off our wood floors. But, there never was a doubt that we would keep them. Whenever I wrote in my cabin and saw the two dogs snuggled at my feet, I found my bliss.

Healing Stories

Crossing the Story Bridge

You can change your life
by changing your story.
—SJF, age 68

"**R**emember a time when you felt challenged or hurt but developed strength or resilience as a result. Then share that with your partner." My reaction was instantaneous.

I know which story wants to be spoken, but I'm not sure I'm ready to share it. It's so humiliating. People deal with terrible things—real trauma—yet, I'm, still clinging to a story from when I was 12 about dancing school.

I had come to this one-day Story Bridge workshop to learn how the director, Dr. Richard Geer, helped communities to build "a play in a day." I had talked to clients for years about how we live within stories and how we can change our lives by changing our stories. I hoped Richard's workshop would give me additional skills to use with others. I didn't anticipate that I'd end up healing a deep wound of mine in the process.

At 9 am, 40 activists, artists, and storytellers gathered in the Whidbey Institute's main hall. Richard told us that we'd start by sharing our personal stories in pairs and then gradually work toward performing eight stories that night for the community. Seeing the worried looks on our faces, Richard assured us that it was doable.

To ease our tension and prepare us for imaginative work, we did 30 minutes of easy physical and improv exercises. Then, he said, "Pick a partner and decide who will be an apple and who will be an orange." I chose an 80-year-old man whom I knew from other workshops, and we decided I would be the apple. At that point, Richard instructed the apples to remember a difficult moment that had helped us to grow. I wondered if this was the time finally to open up about one of my most humiliating moments. I looked into my partner's eyes. They were open and unjudging. I went for it, speaking what I had never told anyone:

I came into the world a dancer. My parents folk danced, and they took me to events where my father dressed in embroidered shirts from Slovenia, and my mother wore colorful skirts from Poland. When I was seven, they dressed me in a red Swiss dirndl and apron-fronted skirt and took me to family day at Folk Dance House in Manhattan. We all stood in a circle, and I held hands with my best friend Toni while we learned to dance the "Mayim Mayim" from Israel and the "Miserlou" from Greece.

When we were ten, Toni and I began making up our own dances. We ran around her four-story wooden house choreographing songs from West Side Story. *We hung off mahogany banisters as if they were the fire exits of tenement buildings and pretended to be the play's star-crossed lovers. We performed high-action kicks in her living room like the Sharks and the Jets getting ready to rumble.*

Because dancing was my thing, I couldn't wait for the start of ballroom lessons at Mr. Walter Schalk's Dance Academy. Schalk, a swanky Fred Astaire wannabe, taught us the moves then in vogue: the foxtrot, waltz, cha-cha, rhumba, and tango. He even offered a bit of jitterbug and promised more if we signed up for his lively musical comedy dance classes.

On my fifth-grade Thursday afternoons, I prepped for class by putting on a starched cotton shirt, an A-line skirt, knee socks, and patent leather Mary Janes. I stuck a pair of the white gloves we girls were required to wear in my pocket.

Schalk promoted his programs to local boys and their parents by promising that ballroom dancing would improve their football skills. Despite his strong pitch, classes always drew 50 percent more girls than boys.

At the beginning of each session, Schalk separated us. He taught the boys, while a fleet of aspiring Ginger Rogerses—tall, thin high school seniors—taught the girls. My years of folk dancing made it easy for me to pick up all the steps.

When Schalk was satisfied with the progress of both groups, he asked the boys and girls to sit in rows facing each other across the gymnasium. Then, like a broadcaster at the races, he announced, "Gentlemen, take your partners." A small army of gawky, pimply-faced, "do-I-really-have-to-be-here" boys left their chairs and began a slow march across the floor toward the girls. A few "cool" boys strode boldly, making sure they had first pick of the most popular girls—like Tina, with her dimples and cheerleader enthusiasm. The rest of the boys surveyed the remaining girls as if we were chattel and continued to pick.

"Pick me, pick me, I know how to dance," I silently screamed, while trying not to look too eager. I tugged on my skirt, crossed and uncrossed my legs, looked at the clock, and hoped no one would hear my heart pounding.

After the last boy had picked his partner, reality and shame descended. I sat in the row with the other leftovers, wishing I could become invisible or self-eject out of the room. None of us still sitting looked at each other. Why acknowledge that we had a neon "not picked" sign blinking behind us? I fumed as I watched the group.

I am a much better dancer than any of them are. How did this happen? What's wrong with me? Maybe if I was pretty, or popular, or more normal . . .

In the second round, Billy Baldwin, the class geek, picked me. Billy couldn't dance, but he liked me because I was smart and talked to him in school. Still humiliated but relieved to be dancing, I fed Billy hints about the steps by applying gentle (or maybe not-so-gentle) pressure to his shoulders. Then, Miss Kelly, the queen of the Ginger Rogers wannabes, walked over and tapped me on the shoulder. "Dear, girls don't lead," she scolded.

I wanted to sock her! But, instead, I stuffed this anger, frustration, and sadness into my overflowing shame sack.

Each Thursday, the scene repeated itself. I'd sit there, anticipating the worst so I wouldn't be disappointed. Later, in high school and beyond, I stayed away from all events where there might be "picking," whether at a street dance or a formal ball.

Not even a turtleneck could cover the R for "rejected" that life had tattooed on my neck.

I wrapped up my story and glanced at my partner. The loving look on his face told me I'd been truly heard, and I breathed a sigh of relief.

Richard then told the "oranges" to repeat the story they'd just heard and to speak it in the first person, as if it were their own. As I listened to my partner share my story without a trace of judgment, I felt a wave of compassion for the little girl. She'd been hurt, as so many of us are in childhood. She was not defective.

After a pause, my partner and I switched roles. I listened to him, then gave him back his story. I glanced around the room and saw twosomes leaning toward each other and talking like intimate pals. Compassion lingered thick in the air as Richard gave us our next assignment: "As a pair, find two other pairs, and form a group of six. Each person will tell their story again, and, after hearing all six stories, the group will pick one to perform tonight in front of the audience."

To my surprise, the group of six picked my story to perform. As we rehearsed, my tale took on a life of its own. We blocked out our entrances, exits, and transitions using Richard's directorial suggestions.

Then, the eight stories from our large group were woven into a "play." Many of them touched on common themes like loss, humiliation, shame, resilience, and gratitude. One focused on the regret of a 50-year-old man for his time in a gang, another on a woman who had felt manipulated by the mother she now had to care for, and another on a young man who had struggled before coming out as an artist in his family. Secrets that had lived as private wounds were woven into a tapestry of what it is to be human.

Our small group performance went well until a blind woman missed her cue and launched her story before ours had ended. I had wanted my little fifth-grade self to be able to dance again. No matter. Her shame had already started to lift.

Back to the Gym

After sharing my story at Story Bridge, I no longer believed I had to hide it. But I sensed I still had more healing to do.

So, six months later, I asked my imagination to help me. As I sat in my cabin one morning, I lit some candles, took a comfortable seat, and closed my eyes. I transported myself back to the gymnasium at the New Canaan High School. I saw a ten-year-old girl sitting in her A-line skirt and scuffed Mary Janes, holding back tears while her anger boiled. As a 68-year-old friend, I walked into the gym and slowly approached her. She was startled when she saw me.

"May I sit down?" I asked. She nodded yes as she stared at the floor. I saw drops of tears on her dress but said nothing. After we'd sat quietly for a bit, I asked, "Can I sit here and tell you a story?"

She glanced at me and nodded as if to say, "If you must."

I took her hand, and she let it rest in mine as I began. "First, I want to tell you I can travel in time. One day, you will be able to as well. And, when I travel back in time, I see a pretty little girl who was excited to go to dancing school but felt so hurt because the boys in her class didn't pick her. She felt ashamed and couldn't understand why they didn't want to partner with her when she was an excellent dancer. She decided that something was terribly wrong with her and that she would be doomed for life."

She glanced at me for a moment.

"In other circumstances, that little girl might have just run out of the room and been able to scream, cry, or get a hug from someone who could have listened and comforted her. Maybe someone could have reminded her what a great dancer she was or invited her to dance. But instead, all the girl could do was sit quietly, pinned to her seat. She prayed to be invisible while she continued to seethe."

"Seethe?" Her brow wrinkled.

"Sorry. It means bundling up your feelings as if you're holding a fire inside and the smoke is filling you."

She nodded.

I continued. "You see, that little girl was a natural dancer—it was as if dance lived in her. When she had to sit there and not dance, she felt that the world didn't see her or care about who she really was. That made her feel so bad."

Again, she nodded.

"Somebody else might have stopped dancing. But, you know what that little girl did? She never stopped. As a girl, she choreographed dances in her living room. Then, as she grew older, she discovered she could dance by herself or with friends at parties and classes. Sometimes, she would dance in front of her windows at night, watching the reflection of her movements and loving what she saw. Later, as an adult, she took classes where she could dance with the woman she saw in the mirror. The two of them would smile and move together with so much joy."

The little girl riveted her eyes on me.

I paused. "Can I tell you something else, even if you might not understand?"

She pursed her lips. "Yes."

"Dance was her special gift. It was part of how God spoke to her. When she danced, she felt Spirit entering her body as if a great force beyond her was guiding her movements. I don't expect you to understand, but I wanted you to know."

"But I do," she said quietly. "It's like that for me, too." Then, she paused and thought. "That little girl is me, right?"

I nodded.

"And the boys?"

"Darling, they were just boys. It was hard for them too. They also worried about being rejected and laughed at. The man you will marry had a hard time at his dancing school. But the good news is that the world will start changing. Boys will no longer get to do all the picking. And you will be free to dance with anyone."

Tears were running down her face.

"You'll dance with your friends and a boy with Down Syndrome. You'll dance with boys and girls—and people who don't care whether they are boys or girls. In Africa, you will dance with new friends of many colors. And one day, you'll dance with a very nice older man with no memory and make his day. And when people watch you dance, they will feel happy."

Tears continued to drip down the edge of her nose, but she was smiling. I put my left arm around her. "Honey, one day, you'll attend your 40th high school class reunion when you're near my age, which might seem old to you now. And there, you will dance as you always wanted to dance. You'll dance with your husband, your friends, and your favorite person—you—as you look into the mirror. You'll notice how the light flows through you. And believe me, you'll be hot!"

She laughed as she threw herself into my arms, trembling. I held her, letting her shake.

"You are the dance, my darling, and no one can ever take that from you." I held her until her body calmed and her sobs turned to sniffles. I gave her the one tissue I had, and she blew her nose loudly.

Then, we got up and walked hand in hand out of the gymnasium hall.

Dancing Like a Bumblebee

Aging had given me permission to express more of myself and claim my dance, my private conversation with Spirit.
—SJF, AGE 69

What to wear? I scoured my closet and headed toward my regulars: blue jeans and a gray cotton sweater. But a Muse-like voice interrupted me as I was pulling on my pants. *"No gray! Go for color, wear stretch, and get ready to dance!"* A pair of bright amber leggings cried, "ME ME ME!" Some fashion experts would say that women over 60, having lost—or never had—tight-as-Jennifer-Lopez-butts, don't belong in stretchy leggings. *Screw them. So what if I'm 69?* No paparazzi would be covering this barbeque fundraiser, and leggings offered me freedom to move to a favorite band that would be there. Remarkably, a matching yellowy-amber sweater also appeared. Had I worn a black vest, I could have passed for a bumblebee.

When we got to the fundraiser, the band was playing in the open meadow just outside the massive white catering tent. No one was dancing yet, but I didn't want to waste any opportunities. I felt the music pulling me, looked at the grassy "dance floor," and thought, *Here I go!* I tossed my purse at my husband, calling out, "Darling, could you get us some seats?" as I trotted away. After so many years together, I knew that he'd be happier watching me than going out on the floor himself.

I had two friends in the band, and I knew how energizing it was for them when people began to dance. I stood before them, moving slowly, jutting my hips to the side and back, as if I were "just listening." But, within seconds, I stopped holding back, raised my arms to make circles in the air, and let loose. Because no one had joined me yet, I had plenty of room to move. I could sway, spin, sashay, and salsa without fear of hitting anyone. As I buzzed about with joy, I noticed the guitar player smiling, as if my movement was reinforcing his creative spark. Within a few minutes, other dancers joined me, and before the call to dinner rang, our grassy venue was packed.

During a break, the band's leader came up to me and said, "I loved watching you. You really express our music when you dance." I wasn't trolling for praise, but that was perhaps the nicest thing anyone had ever said about my dancing. I knew he'd seen what happened when music took me over. I went into a zone where I felt both lifted out of myself and deeply connected to myself. I felt free; I didn't care about the size of my butt or what people might think of me. Aging had given me permission to express more of myself and claim my dance, my private conversation with Spirit.

The little girl from dancing school whispered in my ear that night, *"Someday I'm going to be bolder, too."*

Art, Interrupted

Finding Dad's Art Supplies

One of the beliefs that had limited my creative work for decades was the idea that I was not an artist, or at least not a visual artist. My husband disagreed. "Don't your ikebana arrangements and garden designs qualify as art?"

"That's different," I'd reply, holding tight to a story that began in third grade, when it became evident that I couldn't draw. Some kids, like Toni Squitieri, Susan Hart, and Mark Guerrero—the "real artists"—drew faces that looked like actual people and earned A's in art class. Their drawings and paintings hung on our school walls while I struggled to draw stick figures. Then, when I was ten, I received a B in art class—an obvious failure in our super-competitive school system. With that, I decided to stick to subjects I had a chance of mastering. Leave art to the artistic ones.

My father was an artist. When he reimmersed himself in art later in life, he began living with a small pouch of supplies strapped to his well-worn brown belt. In it, he carried a pen, a bottle of water-soluble black ink, a tiny vial of water, and a mini-notebook. When he and Mom toured Europe as sixtysomethings, he sketched in cafes. When they went to the ocean, he drew unsuspecting bathers while he sat in a low beach chair with his feet in the sand.

When Dad got cancer at 82, his art-making dwindled. My parents decided to move to a small bungalow in a retirement center that Mom would be able to maintain after he died, so he packed up the bedroom he had called his studio. He placed his art supplies in a large cardboard box, along with dozens of mini-sketchbooks he had filled with pictures of church towers, river scenes, street life, gardens, clocks, bathers, and children playing.

Two years after Dad died, Mom asked for help cleaning out her garage. Among the boxes of outdated toxic cleaning supplies, braided lanyards and similar "gifts" from her children's camp days, and outdated sewing patterns, I discovered Dad's art supplies. They sat on a high shelf, wedged between scrapbooks and photo albums.

I hoisted the heavy box and set it on the floor. I resisted opening it, remembering how private Dad had been about his creative projects. When my curiosity got the better of me, I reached in and discovered a set of shoe boxes, each meticulously organized. One held his varnishes and cleaners. Another revealed a bottle of linseed oil, mat cutters, pen knives, and a pen nib—a pointed, quill-like object to be used with a jar of India ink. One box contained dark charcoals and a set of professional-grade flesh-colored pastels.

The last box was marked "watercolors" and held his crown jewels, stored in small Windsor Newton boxes, each marked with the name of a color family: red, yellow, green, violet, and black. In that moment, I realized that my dad must have loved color. I would have never suspected that, given the selection of gray suits he wore throughout his career. Yet, the tubes I found in his boxes had labels with alluring names I didn't recognize: yellow gamboge, cerulean blue, carmine red, phthalo green.

The supplies were technically Mom's, so I returned to the house where she sat in her embroidered rocking chair watching TV. "Mom, I just found the box of Dad's art supplies. Do you know what you'd like to do with them?"

She looked up at me quizzically and said, "I don't know. What do you think? Maybe give them to an artist like Michael?" Michael was my cousin's son who was studying painting.

"Yeah, maybe. I'll do something," I mumbled, while thinking, *Absolutely not, no way. Dad's supplies carry his essence, and they are coming home with me! Someday I'll use them.*

I drove back to the island that night with a trove of art supplies in the trunk of my car. The next day, I took a stick of charcoal out of one of the boxes and swiped it across a sheet of paper. My fingers became covered in soot as I watched a bold arc emerge.

If art making includes playing and putting marks on a page, maybe I'll have a chance.

But, after living for a few days with my dad's old supplies scattered across our dining room table, that thought subsided. I repackaged the box and placed it in a closet, where it sat for the next 17 years.

"But, I'm Not an Artist"

If you hear a voice within you say, "You cannot paint,"
then by all means, paint, and that voice will be silenced.
—ATTRIBUTED TO VINCENT VAN GOGH

*E*ven as I explored different creative expressions, I stayed attached to my story that I wasn't a visual artist. Artists observed the world through their eyes; I used my mind to play with words and ideas. If I was attending a retreat, and someone announced we'd be doing an arts and crafts project, I'd cringe and try to disappear—until one day, when a woman refused to believe my story.

When I first met Geri at a friend's Christmas party, I was drawn to her sparkling eyes and impish warmth. Her husband, Jack, a colleague from a writing class, had shared some of my work with Geri and wanted to introduce us. I noticed her hands bouncing about. "Can you tell I have tremors?" She laughed. Judging by her wrinkled face and long gray hair, I assumed she was in her late seventies, but when she talked about her love of watercolors, her face lit up, and she looked much younger. She commented on my writing and asked, "What are you working on now?"

"Living a more creative life after 50," I responded.

Her eyes widened. "I should tell you my story. I worked for years at Boeing. After I retired, my sister talked me into going to a watercolor class. I didn't want to go, but I did it for her. I fell in love with watercolors, and within a few years, I was teaching. It's been 20 years now, and even my tremors can't stop me from painting!" She grinned and added, "Why don't you come to my class at the Senior Center? You don't have to know anything about art. I think you'd love it."

I was ready with my customary deflection. "Thanks, Geri, but I don't do art. I write, but I can't draw or paint." Besides, I thought to myself, my life was already too full.

Geri stared at me expectantly, like a puppy who doesn't understand the expressions "Down" and "No." "You'll like class. Lots of us have been beginners. Why don't you try it?"

We talked a little longer before I moved to the food table and gorged on some stuffed grape leaves. Out of nowhere, Isabel appeared, and, quite uncharacteristically, demanded my attention.

"Why do you keep saying no to art? You've kept your father's art supplies for 17 years, saying you'd use them someday. When is this 'someday'? When you get old? Don't you qualify yet?" (She laughed.) *"What could be less risky than Geri's class? Give it a try."*

This was a pushy side of Isabel I'd rarely seen. She didn't pull her punches when she added: *"Or let go of those art supplies."*

Yaow! But maybe she was right. I thought about my father's love for watercolors, and I wondered if he would have been willing to teach me about them.

Steve interrupted my ruminations with a signal that it was time for us to leave. We thanked our hosts, then walked to the door to pull on our winter boots before heading out into the snow. Steve whispered, "Why not take Geri's class?"

Geri saw us and waved. "Will I see you?"

I paused. "OK. Yeah. I'll be there." She grinned, and I left the party shell-shocked, an unexpected tear forming at the corner of my eye.

On the day of my first class with Geri, I took Dad's box of art supplies out of the closet and lifted the lid. I dug deep to find his treasured watercolors. Some color tubes he had used; others he never opened. I picked five to take to class: burnt sienna, hooker's green, yellow ochre, cadmium orange, and rose madder.

After entering the Senior Center, I joined a group of gray-haired beginners listening to Geri's basic instructions. "You only need three paints and a couple of brushes to start doing watercolors. Buy good paper. And don't worry about mistakes. You see how the tremors help me make mistakes?" She laughed that same infectious laugh I'd heard at the party.

She taught us a technique called "wet on wet," in which we poured wet paint onto wet paper. As I dribbled cadmium orange on my sheet, the color magically started expanding. Then, I poured yellow ochre over it and watched as the colors danced, sometimes merging, sometimes sliding apart. I added rose madder, and the work took on a "look at me!" punch.

If letting paint meander across a wet page is art, maybe I have a chance. You don't have to be good. Just explore art and have fun.

I returned home and ordered a palette, multiple brushes, and a pad of good watercolor paper. Then, walking outside to feed the horses, I saw a world exploding with color. Was sunlight on madrona tree bark burnt sienna, cadmium yellow, or raw umber? Was the sky aquamarine or cobalt? Were clouds pure white or were they flecked with mauve?

Geri had broken the spell. I could no longer say, "I don't do art."

Back inside the house, I caressed Dad's tubes of watercolors. Only now, they were mine. I wanted every shade he had left and more. I craved color.

And, I really missed my dad.

There Are No Mistakes

Children are born into wonder. But as adults,
many of us have to rediscover what we never really lost.
—SJF, AGE 69

I spent several afternoons painting with Geri before the pandemic closed her face-to-face courses. But the lockdown that prevented work in person opened other doors. Dana Lynne Andersen, an artist friend I had met in a virtual seminar two years earlier, started offering her classes online. I couldn't wait to work with her. Having broken the spell of "I don't do art," I wanted to keep learning, but I knew I was too tender for a traditional art class that included "critique." I needed to find joy in making art without trying to make "good art."

Fortunately, Dana did not care at all about the products students made in her classes. In her "transformative arts" approach, she focused on the process of making art by guiding her students toward discovery, growth, and spiritual connection. She encouraged movement, play, and finding the magic within messes. I devoured the words on her website: "The act of creating is an opening through which the infinite can enter." And, "True creativity is an act of turning inward, and *expressing* or '*pressing out*' from the vast resources of the inner realms."

Still, I needed to reassure myself before I enrolled in a class, so I called her. "Dana, I'm a recovering non-artist, and I don't know anything. I haven't made art in 50-plus years."

She laughed. "It doesn't matter. Lots of my students come with similar stories—it's the culture these days. By third grade, something happens to many kids in school, and they decide they can't make art. You don't have to worry; just come and play."

"Yeah, but I don't even understand the materials list. What are tempera paints? And acrylics? And what do I do about brushes? And paper?"

I didn't have time to order supplies before class, but Dana put me at ease, saying, "Any water-based paint you can pour is great. Cheap tempera is fine. Or use whatever you have—even coffee grinds." (Which turned out later to be a favorite medium.) "Or rip pictures out of magazines. Break apart old boxes if you don't have anything to paint or collage on."

I dove into Dad's art box and found a few tubes of acrylic paints that I could mix with water and pour. For paper, I found a flip chart pad—big and cheap, and, it turned out, not sturdy enough to support work with water. It didn't matter. At the start of class, Dana said, "Don't worry about the materials. If your paper bunches or tears, make that part of your art. If your paper is too expensive, you won't feel free."

In Dana's world, there were no mistakes. If I didn't like what I did, I could throw my work away, start over, or cut it up to use in a future collage. She started class off with music, suggesting that we move our bodies as she led us in meditation. "Feel the energy in your body. Move your pelvis. Sway like seaweed." I bent and swayed, moving my hands in big circles, alternating between reaching down to the earth and up toward the stars. Then, Dana invited us to return to our painting stations. "Keep moving. Touch your sheet and run your hands over it. Slosh some water on the paper, and feel where it wants to go."

I watched the water run to the edges of my flip chart paper, then poured a little watered-down aquamarine acrylic over it. Little bubbles of color swam across the sheet like amoebas. Next, I added magenta and watched purple puddles merge into the blue. Then, I dripped drops of yellow, but I didn't like the murky brown that emerged from the mix.

I moved paints with a brush, my breath, a credit card, and my fingers. (Fingers were my favorite!) When I felt satisfied with my first piece of work, I lifted it and laid it on the floor to dry. The paint continued to move around, which changed the design—good training for letting go and embracing chaos. I remembered Dana's message: "There are no mistakes."

I took out another sheet of paper and filled it with the bold strokes of chalk pastels—another gift from Dad—stepping back occasionally to observe what I had created. Chalk welcomed big gestures and large sweeps of color. Then I took out another sheet and experimented again with paint. Soon, I saw four sheets full of lines, blobs, and colors staring back at me as if they had something to say.

At the end of class, we each worked with a partner and explored through dance, sound, or poetry what our pieces might tell us. I loved this dialogue, and by the time class ended, I felt exhausted and alive.

That night, as I dreamed, aquamarine, yellow, and magenta danced in front of my eyes.

"Art Is a Stance Toward Life"

*Your job is to keep returning to the place
that feels most alive in you and nurturing that.*
—MARCO

I had to pinch myself whenever I stood at my painting table and realized I could play with the materials. Marco particularly loved visual art, and he reached out to support me, saying,

> "Behind our work and play lives a spark. We nurture it by giving thanks and honoring its magic—then letting it expand us. The spark works through us, but it is not ours. When we forget that, our art becomes hollow.
> "Your job is to keep returning to the place that feels most alive in you and nurturing that."

I began spending hours playing with paints and pencils. Most days, I'd be delighted with my experiments, but occasionally, I'd end up discouraged, feeling as if I didn't have a clue what I was doing. For a brief moment, I'd lament that I didn't have design skills and wonder why I was adding visual art to a palette of creative activities that was already too full.

Yet, at the same time, I saw that joy seemed to beget joy, and I appreciated the synergies emerging amongst my different expressions.

Whenever I painted with Dana, I found myself writing and editing in a way that felt more relaxed and effective than usual. Or, when I headed to the garden after sketching, I saw the forms in front of me in new ways. Marco invited me to think differently about art-making:

"Art is not a thing we do but a stance toward life. It is a looking and finding, a dreaming, a seeing and shaping, a listening and a sound. Art allows the future to speak to us through the imagination, the part of us that can hear before the mind can understand. Art lives in the flow when we allow the universe to vibrate within us and move us in ways we couldn't have predicted.

"The art you seek lives within your heart as a mystery worthy of expression. You give it form. You must always work in service to that mystery, even as you develop your craft.

"Not all art comes from Spirit, but why not always seek that possibility? As we do, our creating can create us. Our eyes open to a new world, and we hear the voice of our Longing.

"Then, we can shiver with the possibility that we are being guided."

Designing Days

Devoted Discipline

*It's one thing to fall in love with the idea of creating. It's
another thing to spend the hours needed to weave what
you love into your life and cement it into your bones.*
—MARCO

By the time I was 70, creative expression played a starring role in
my life. But that expression didn't just take the form of making
art or writing; it manifested itself in how I designed and created my
life every day.

Returning from Japan, I'd been delighted to experiment with my
new creative practices. Then, as some appealed to me more—ikebana,
gardening, writing, and art—I wanted to move beyond experimenting.
I wanted to study. Over the next few years, these expressions began to
feel like my "work," which I defined as "the activities to which I am
passionately committed," sidestepping the question of whether I was
paid. (Generally, I was not.)

After hours of freewriting, I wanted to craft better sentences. After
happily planting anything, I wanted to understand what grew best in
the Northwest. After throwing paint on a sheet of paper, I was curious
which colors combined best. But to develop skills, I needed to practice
regularly, and for that, I needed discipline.

I knew that to some people, the word "discipline" sounded like a
downer, as in "to discipline a child" or "to take disciplinary action." To

me, discipline meant showing up for what I cared about and asking myself the question: *Am I applying myself to what has heart and meaning to me?* Discipline helped me balance out the parts of my personality that could be free-spirited and disorganized. It kept me focused on what I cared most about.

Marco reminded me: *"It's one thing to fall in love with the idea of creating. It's another thing to spend the hours needed to weave what you love into your life and cement it into your bones."*

The writer Annie Dillard suggested something similar when she wrote, "How we spend our days is, of course, how we spend our lives," as she made the case for schedules. I created a scaffolding of support for my work with intentions, goals, schedules, routines, and rhythms. But the foundation for everything I did lay in my devotion to what I was doing.

I drew inspiration from stories about the famed cellist Pablo Casals. When he was in his mid-nineties, he still played Bach every afternoon in his Puerto Rican home. I imagined that the man who described Bach's cello suites as shining with a "glittering kind of poetry" rarely had to force himself to practice.

My friend Lori once told me, "Create what you love, and love what you create." This helped me when my gremlins threatened to suck the life out of what I was doing. Despite my commitment to valuing process more than product, I wasn't immune to bouts of wicked self-judgment. I noticed that when I worried about people's reactions to my writing, it went flat—at least for a moment. Even positive criticism felt fraught. I felt good if friends visited my studio and commented on a piece of art that they liked. But then, I'd almost instantly wonder, *Why didn't they like the other pieces?* If they entered and said nothing, I'd ask, *What did I do wrong?* Or, if they enthused about my work, I'd think, *Oh, jeez, I'll never meet their standards in the future.*

As I headed toward completion of this book, the gremlins became very noisy, chanting, *"No one besides your friends will read it."* Their comments, together with the ever-discouraging news from the publishing industry, could send me to Steve, whining, "It's no use."

He'd have to say, "Haven't you read your own book? I thought you said you were writing because . . ."

"Yeah, I know. I write because I love the process of writing. Because I feel called. Because not writing the book would make me feel like I've shorted my life."

"Right. So, does it matter whether you're read by thousands?"

"Well, I'd like that."

"But . . ."

"That's not why I keep writing."

His guidance always helped. So were Isabel's questions:

~ Am I doing the creative work that calls to me?

~ Am I finding joy?

~ Am I loving what I'm doing?

Her questions became my shield when the gremlins attacked. I could counteract their killjoy spirit with one sentence: *"Thank you for your thoughts, but I'm doing this work because I love it."*

That always shut them up. Gremlins don't know how to counter love.

Flowing with Focus

Your creative work won't stand up for
itself if you don't stand up for it.
—Marco

*D*evotion gave me motivation; discipline invited me to show up for work.

I considered my calendar a friend, but it was also a tough master. Each week, I looked at my schedule to see what blocks of time were available for writing, painting, or playing. When I wanted to write for 20 hours but had only five unscheduled hours during the week, my calendar would ask, "How is that going to work?" And when I was able to block a two-hour session of writing, painting, or gardening into my schedule in advance, it made me happy. Even if my week looked busy, that block would stand out like an oasis.

Like any human, I had only 24 hours in a day and often felt like I needed more. Even my creative expressions competed with each other for time. When I was in the midst of intense editing, I could feel guilty that the garden needed work. When I devoted myself to art, I didn't give my writing the attention it deserved. When I gardened, I didn't give my horse her needed regular exercise. I could exhaust myself just thinking about such conflicts.

I laughed at the '60s adage, "Just go with the flow," which meant relax, chill, and coast down the river of life. But I had too many rivers to choose from, with enough passions, interests, and responsibilities to fill two lifetimes. I had to decide which current I wanted to flow in and then navigate around the boulders of distraction that could topple me from my raft.

A billion-dollar advertising and social media industry was betting against my ability to sustain my focus in the face of its seductive headlines, tempting stories, and copious buying opportunities. If I jumped into the stream of the morning news, I could end up capsized in a bog of gloom before breakfast, my mind swimming in accounts of the latest injustice or titillating pop culture revelation.

Each day, I could feel overwhelmed just looking at my to-dos in the morning. Sometimes I wondered whether they had been breeding at night. Much of my list was the stuff of life: taxes, doctors' appointments, client billings, house cleaning, Steve's medical needs. And, even when I thought I had an elegant plan for the day, there were always the "what can go wrongs." When I had a morning set aside for writing, I'd snuggle into my chair only to discover that the internet was down, requiring a call to the provider. Or my software had to be updated and my password was nowhere to be found. Or the furnace repair man would call to say that he was finally on his way over.

I tried to keep an ongoing mantra of gratitude going for what I was able to do, knowing that I'd never do all that I would like. I spent time before bed reviewing what had gone well, what had delighted me, and what I was grateful for. The question "Did I find joy?" was more helpful than "Did I do everything I had hoped?"—the answer to which was almost always, "No."

Planning "Lite"

Your creative spirit comes through in how
you plan as well as what you do.
—Isabel

*H*ow I planned and designed my days was becoming as important as what I did. After all, I was inventing my life—my most creative task of all. I experimented with using intentions, schedules, and routines as a way to avoid relying on a resource I no longer had much of: willpower.

In my thirties and forties, I attended high-priced personal growth seminars that preached the gospel of accountability. We were told to "live as our word"—that is to say, to honor all of our commitments. While this was inspiring to me, over time, I became more jaded. Thinking back on all the motivational talks I had heard, I realized that most of the "preachers" were usually over-hyped coaches under 40. I wondered whether they softened their pitch after 20 more years of life. What would happen to their "do or die" commitments if they received a call telling them that their mother was in the ER and might not have much longer to live? Or if they were stranded in bed with a severe case of brain fog that set in with the pandemic and never left?

Then, they might have been willing to accept some of *my* advice. "Have a life. The world is not that controllable. And you're aging, for heaven's sake! Can't you cut yourself some slack already? Pick planning tools that fit the life you are living now."

With Isabel's inspiration, I looked for ways to plan that fit where I was in my life. I was no longer interested in setting big "stretch" goals. Just living was stretching me enough, thank you. And I didn't want to design my creative life using mechanistic business planning tools. I preferred to incorporate colors, squiggles, lines, and movement to make my scheduling process itself expressive. I completed collages and vision boards to draw forth my dreams for the future. I experimented with automatic writing in the hopes that an inspiring new idea might pop through. I played music to enter a state where dreams could come to me, and I used movement to see my ideas take on gestural forms.

I rarely made rigidly defined goals, such as, "I will finish writing this chapter by Wednesday noon," unless such an objective inspired my work. When I made goals, I tried to stay away from tight metrics, despite having once taught that planning needed to include measurable results. Phrases like *"I intend for my writing to help others expand their creative freedom,"* inspired, but *"One thousand people will buy my book during the first month after publication"* did not.

I still wanted to meet my commitments. At the same time, I wasn't interested in beating myself up when one of the multiple balls I had in the air fell to Earth and splattered. When I was worried about Steve's health, my brain scrambled, and I forgot things. When I was upset, I tended to create chaos and drop my belongings around the house. The piles on my desk grew, and I never quite found the time to clean my office. These were signs that I needed to slow down and refocus. I thought about what Marco had told me, that *"Art is a stance toward life,"* not an obligation to run a particular schedule.

Along with my devotion, I had a superpower, if you can call it that: my resolve. It had inspired me to complete my dissertation when I was working full-time. It had helped me through the process of designing and launching a university graduate program. It had supported me to meet my magazine deadlines, even when I started out thinking I had little to say.

My resolve was not fueled by motivation or even accountability. I persevered when I felt called and committed to what I was doing. The fuel I needed most was love. As Marco constantly reminded me, *"Devote yourself to what you are doing, and let that inspire all of your creations."*

Rhythms and Routines

To give yourself to your creative work is no small feat. It demands a sacrifice, a discipline, a turning away from the demands of the parts of life that claw at you with pseudo-importance. The world is intent on distracting us from who we are, seducing us with attractions, offers, and entertainments. We risk losing the holiness of our days and our precious moments to create.
—Marco

We humans like rhythms. In fact, I believe our metabolism was built to expect them. We followed the beat of our mothers' hearts and then listened to our own. We inhale rhythmically and then exhale. We expect darkness to move into day and spring to head toward fall. We move naturally from a period of activity into a time of rest.

While life's rhythms are baked into us, the "constantly on" aspect of the internet is creating a culture that seems increasingly arrhythmic. We no longer have to step away from the computer at midnight, and if we're up at 2 am, we can order a book or washing machine. In some cities (but not on my island!), we can order take-out food around the clock. In a world that's always on, we run the risk of divorcing ourselves from the rhythms of the natural world and forgetting how steadying it can be to live life with a predictable beat.

In my university position, rhythms and routines were given to me. Monday afternoons were for staff meetings. Tuesday mornings, I attended the tedious-but-obligatory bickering session known as the all-faculty council. Wednesdays, I joined the executive committee for the weekly budget fight. I usually taught on Thursday nights or weekends—the most satisfying part of my schedule. Semester breaks, holidays, and vacations punctuated the year.

When I left that job, I lost some of its tedious and obligatory aspects. But I also lost its rhythms. When I started working for myself, I had to find patterns that supported my days; no employer was doing it for me. When I cut back on my consulting work at 64 to focus on creative pursuits, I found myself awash in the terrifying freedom of mostly unstructured time. I lost the boundaries that had defined the workday and had to impose my own, like, "Stop work by 7 pm." Weekends looked increasingly like weekdays.

Although I didn't want to be driven by commitments to others, I missed having a few deadlines to punctuate my week. So, I created one for myself: the goal of publishing a blog post every Thursday at 2 pm. That target gave a pulse to the week—an arc of anticipation, tension, progress, and completion. If I didn't have a blog topic by Wednesday, my anxiety would surge just enough to help birth an idea. Without a fixed cutoff, I would have worried about whether or not my themes were blog-worthy. But having a time limit forced me to make choices and move ahead, despite my hesitations.

When I pushed the "publish" button on Thursday, I could yell to my husband—my faithful copy editor—"I just hit 'send'!" That was our moment for a high-five and brief celebration; we had met the week's small challenge. Since I was rarely rewarded with paychecks, contracts, or outside acknowledgment for my work, our little in-home victory parties meant a lot to me.

Working for myself allowed me the opportunity to match what I was doing to the energy I had. The early parts of my day worked best for mental activity; I was most clear-headed and ready for the cognitive effort writing required. When that clarity waned, I switched to more mundane activities like doing laundry, making appointments, or following up on emails. In the afternoon, I returned to editing or to less demanding activities, like watching a webinar to learn about book marketing.

I wasn't always good about stopping, although my body was happiest when I took time in the afternoon to garden, walk, or move around. When I could paint in the late afternoon or evening, that activity often revived me.

I found having a few routines was helpful. They kept me from having to ask, *What shall I do now?* My 30-year-old self would not have understood why I liked routines, for she considered anything repetitious to be boring. (Apparently, my personality type needs change to thrive.) But, by 60, my life was so full of stimulation that having some predictability and a few patterns felt good. I could fall into a groove and be carried where I needed to go.

Some creativity consultants advocate seeking variety—like taking a new route home from work every day. But my life was overfilling with differences begging to be noticed. Every time I walked through the woods, the world looked different with branches down, ground covers growing, and bushes beginning to bud. I could feed my creativity by noticing life in the forest.

So, contrary to the experts' advice, I sought more constancy. When I kept parts of my life simple, I could channel more energy into my creative endeavors. I learned about this strategy from my doctoral committee chair. She held our meetings over lunch at the same restaurant each month, at the same time, and, preferably, at the same table. She ordered Chinese chicken salad, never pausing to consider a Cobb salad or a Mexican tortilla-salad special. She chose not to waste time on small decisions. Her creative powers were reserved for expeditiously steering me through the dissertation process, not food selection.

Twenty-five years after our work together ended, her logic still spoke to me. Small decisions bombarded me regularly, and I wanted fewer of them. When my electric toothbrush died, I could spend hours research-ing replacement options before picking one. Looking for a non-violent movie to stream could take more time than watching it. Even choosing a laundry detergent tapped my finite decision-making powers.

I was most successful creating a routine for myself in the morning. I woke up typically between 5:30 (early) and 7:30 am (late). My reward for an early rise was a pre-dawn concert by the trilling white-crowned sparrows. Then, I'd stagger into the kitchen, put on a kettle of water, and begin my ritual tea-making. I drank lime water when I had the fruit because I heard it was good for me. But more than that, the scent of citrus sent me back to my days living in tropical Ecuador, if only for a moment.

After a first cup of tea, it was time to meditate, usually on the couch. My motto about meditation was "anything is better than nothing," even if my meditation posture was not yoga-endorsed. (I'm stiff in the morning.) I used different forms of meditation, enjoying embodiment techniques that reminded me that I had an amazing physical container to dwell in before I plunged into my more cerebral work.

On days without morning obligations away from home, I followed meditation with a trip to the cabin to write. The 30-second walk outside the house provided just enough time to enjoy the seasonal smells of pine, honeysuckle, lily, or rose. I tried to ignore the weeds.

After writing for an hour, I fed the horses and mucked their stalls and paddock. Mucking—horse people's term for cleaning—for me was another meditation, and the slow, repetitive lifting of my manure fork gave me time to think about my writing or the day. After completing the job, I'd go back to the house for breakfast and conversation with my husband, then return to the cabin to write for another hour or more while my mind was still alert.

I wasn't able to follow this routine every day, but when I did, it set the tone for the hours to come.

Creating Sanctuary

You are the carpenter building the scaffolding for your creative life. Create a sanctuary to support your heart's work. You will still feel beholden to obligations outside of your control. But your space, your sanctuary, will give you a place to return, a temple that honors your Longing.
—MARCO

Virginia Woolf wrote about needing "a room of one's own." I'm not sure a room is always necessary, but having the right space makes creating so much easier. Because our house was small and my office tiny, Steve and I built the small cabin that became a sanctuary for my writing and meditations as well as a place of respite from the files, emails, projects, and bills that went with my teaching and coaching practice.

Sanctuary: A place of refuge or safety. Synonym: An oasis or haven.

As soon as I crossed the cabin's transom and flicked on the sconces, my mood shifted. The woodsy smell invited contemplation. In winter, I could look out the window at the bare hazelnut branches and imagine their leafing out in spring. In spring, I saw the bleeding hearts emerging in the shade of the "full moon" Japanese maple. In summer, I smelled the sweet honeysuckle as fresh air from open windows filled the cabin.

And, in the fall, I watched the red gum trees in the backyard enjoy their time of glory before gradually losing their leaves.

In any season, sitting in my chair helped me relax and refocus. I credit the cabin with jump-starting my writing.

When it came time to take art classes with Dana, the cabin didn't work as well. It had a fickle internet connection and no room for a table. I did my first paintings at the dining room table, with newspapers spread over the floor to protect against inevitable spills and drips. That worked—until my husband and I tired of pushing aside pots of paint in order to eat lunch.

Steve, who'd supported building the cabin, wasn't keen on devoting any more shared space to my creative pursuits. (In my defense, he claimed dominion over the whole garage.) But, one day, he surprised me by bringing home a scuffed maple table that he installed in the all-purpose/guest room we called "the studio." (Another proof that my husband is a keeper!)

Being able to work at that old table facing the garden transformed my relationship with art. I could leave supplies set up, and then, when I had a free half-hour, walk into the studio where my pencils, paints, brushes, and paper said, "Let's go." I taped my beginner's drawings, chalk work, and paintings on the walls and cabinets so that I could continue my conversations with them.

Some people like to fashion altars to create a sense of sanctuary. The bookcase in my cabin—crammed with books on writing, creativity, and spirituality—was like one to me. When I needed inspiration, I sat on the red faux-Oriental carpet and stared at titles.

Rituals can build a sense of sanctuary as well. I was a bit of a failure in using some of the ones commonly employed by my writer friends. I would ring a Tibetan bell to start my writing period, then forget to ring it again at the close. Once, I lit a candle before beginning to write and then became so absorbed in my work that I left it burning overnight.

The cabin survived, but I decided that, for me, candles worked better as decoration. One practice that did work for me was putting on headphones and streaming instrumental music from a favorite playlist. The right soundtrack could help me reconnect me to a depth within myself, whether or not I kept it going while I wrote.

And my favorite rite of all? Before I left the house to write, I'd call out, "Cabin!" In an instant, two four-footed creatures would greet me at the door. Why they thought it was such a treat to lie on the floor of a 12'x16' writing space I don't know. But having the dogs with me was a ritual that always said, "You're in your happy place, and it's time to begin."

Living with Time

Ben Franklin said, "Time is money," and probably every schoolchild in America has gotten that message. We live in a culture that slices, dices, and measures time in every conceivable way. Our houses are full of time-keeping devices—from thermostats to toothbrushes—counting the minutes in every room.

The Greeks called this measured time "chronos," in honor of one of their gods. It inspired my husband's chronograph watch with its half-dozen dials measuring who-knows-what. When I looked at my remaining years of life through the lens of chronos-time, things didn't look so good. I had fewer and fewer days ahead of me. I worried whether I had enough time to learn to write or publish a book.

Fortunately, the Greeks gave us an alternative, "kairos," named after another god. Kairos is often defined as "right" or "opportune" timing, but I like to think of it as the space I stepped into when I was in the flow of a creative process and my awareness of chronos-time faded away. I'd enter a mysterious and magical zone, only stopping when a piece felt done or told me I could break. When I stepped into kairos-time, I stopped worrying about having enough minutes and instead treasured what I had.

I needed both chronos and kairos in my life. My schedule (chronos) ensured that I made it to appointments and classes and had time in the studio. Once I was there, kairos offered spaciousness and a more time-less experience. While I was still beholden to the clock in most aspects of my life, I could see that time was more mysterious and malleable than I had once imagined.

For example, one day, when I was running very late to a dentist's appointment, I jumped into the car and sped down the driveway. I stopped to open the farm gate that separates the "deer-are-welcome" portion of our property from the "no-deer-parties-here" section. That was when I noticed a young doe and her newborn fawn grazing ten yards ahead. We stared at each other for several seconds, each unsure of what to do. Then, the doe bounded into the woods, leaving her baby. (The doe credo: "Save yourself first.")

I returned to my car and drove cautiously forward, keeping my eyes peeled for the fawn. I spotted her in some long grass, curled up as if she'd already learned how to make herself invisible. She was a brown-and-white fur ball, probably less than a week old. I stopped the car, got out, and approached her slowly, respecting her space by not getting too close or touching her. She lay still, nose quivering, barely breathing. I stood there for a minute, humbled by this precious connection with the wild. Then, I blessed her, returned to the car, and drove slowly out of the driveway. Miraculously, I arrived at the dentist on time. And I never forgot those few moments with the fawn.

The Art of "No-ing"

"*E*deen, I've seen you often, and you seem to know a lot about gardening," I said to the elderly woman walking carefully along the delphinium-lined paths at the home of one our Vashon Garden Club members. "Would you like to join our club?"

She shook her head and smiled. "Thank you. I do love visiting, but I can't be joining anything. I must stay focused on writing."

Right then, this 87-year-old woman became my personal hero. She taught me the importance of making choices and saying no, even to things I loved. So, a year after my term as Garden Club President ended, I regretfully withdrew from the group. I also left the Master Gardener program once the heat from my early gardening days cooled. I cut back on meetings and classes in Seattle, realizing that each trip to the mainland could take the better part of a day. When COVID-19 swept the country, I was one of the lucky ones who relished the requirement not to go anywhere. I used that time to write.

Cutting back was not without consequences. The weeds took over the garden. Because I attended fewer meetings and coffee dates, I worried that I was becoming unsocial. When my "foodie" friends invited me to dinner, I felt like I should reciprocate. But, while cooking was their creative pastime, it wasn't mine. I struggled with how to return their gifts. Occasionally, I found ways to compromise. Once, I invited a friend to celebrate her birthday dinner with us but became grumpy when I realized I might need to choose between cooking and writing that day. Fortunately, inspiration struck, and I realized that I could buy dinners and baklava from the local Syrian food truck. We honored my friend on her birthday with a relaxed and delicious meal, supported a refugee family, and preserved my writing time. This was an example of transforming constraints into possibilities—a skill that I told my leadership students was at the heart of design thinking. Even though "no-ing" didn't come easily to me, it felt great whenever I succeeded at letting go of an unneeded expectation.

Edeen died at 92. I read her obituary and learned that she had published a volume of poetry a few months before her death and had almost finished her memoir. The paper quoted her as once saying, "I am, therefore I write."

Sounding and Silence

Return to the Keyboard

The last event I attended before the pandemic officially hit Washington State in March 2020 was a writing retreat on Whidbey Island with Christina Baldwin and a group of eight other alumni of her "Self as the Source of the Story" workshops—the one I had done five years earlier. We gathered in a large Victorian house overlooking Puget Sound, blissfully oblivious to the curtain that was about to drop on face-to-face gatherings for the next two years. Happily ensconced, we spent our days writing and our evenings feasting and reading to each other. At one of those readings, my new friend Sara shared a beautiful piece that propelled me to revisit my relationship with the piano.

Our group came together, as usual, by circling the altar as someone lit a candle. After we settled in, Sara began reading her essay about taking up the cello after midlife. The moment she described her love for her instrument, she captured my attention, and my mind flooded with thoughts.

I took piano lessons from grade school through high school. Five days a week, I sat at our old upright grand with its broken ivory keys and practiced for 45 minutes. But during college, I quit.

I once loved my piano. Why did I ever stop playing?

Sara described how, during her childhood, her parents never encouraged music, art, or creativity. "I was taught that creativity was an extracurricular activity that never would do the world much good," she read. Her family thought the arts and music were frivolous. "They believed in responsibility, not imagination."

I was luckier. My parents encouraged my piano playing and supported my lessons. They expected me to practice.

I remembered my hours of plunking away at my scuffed old pal, even when part of me wanted to be out in the woods. I'd play Hanon's repetitive piano exercises and scales, learn new work, and try to memorize pieces. I didn't need motivation or goals to support my progress; I just knew how cross my teacher, Mrs. Holcomb, would be if I came to a lesson unprepared. Fortunately, I loved most of the music I played, and I liked feeling how I improved when I practiced.

Mrs. Holcomb was a graduate of the prestigious New England Conservatory of Music and had high standards for her students. She stood by the piano with pursed lips, her white hair pulled tight in a bun, a red pencil always in hand. She filled my sheet music pages with circles surrounding notes I had missed, then added fingering suggestions, phrasing, and comments. When I finally mastered a piece, she drew a red star next to its title. Despite her strictness, Mrs. Holcomb cared deeply about music and tried to share that passion with me. Before assigning me a piece, she would play it, and I would hear the love coming through the nuances and shading she added to even the simplest compositions. She would speak with reverence about the man behind the music—often Bach, Beethoven, Schumann or Shubert—adding a brief story if she had one. When I played at each of her required student recitals, she'd beam with pride and then reward me with a four-inch plaster bust from a collection of famous composers. My parents would congratulate me, and then, back home, I'd introduce the new figure to his companions sitting on top of our piano. By the time I was in high school, I had a complete set, from Albenini to Wagner. My favorite was Brahms—his "Intermezzo in A" was the last piece I learned as a senior in high school.

Sara described how, for years, she had channeled her creativity into teaching children, and later, working as a therapist. She helped others to express their artistic and musical gifts but did little to support her own. Then, Sara began taking women on vision quests into the California wilderness. On one, she had her own vision. In a closing circle, she announced: "I'm going to learn to play the cello." It didn't matter that she was in her late sixties, that the cello was extremely challenging to learn, or that she had never played an instrument and couldn't read music.

I'm grateful I learned to read music, although sight reading is still hard. I always thought I'd play forever. But then . . . what happened?

I remembered what had happened. After high school, I enrolled in Oberlin College, hoping vibes from its famous Conservatory of Music might rub off on me. But in my first week on campus, I discovered that, as a liberal arts student, I would have to audition at the Conservatory if I wanted to take piano lessons. It was a high bar for someone whose only performance experience had been playing before the appreciative parents of her fellow students.

On the afternoon of my audition, I entered the "Con's" darkened hall and sat at a shiny black grand piano in front of two judges. I adjusted the leather bench and sat down as sweat poured down my sides. As I began playing (the Brahms's Intermezzo), a gremlin snuggled next to me and started a running commentary: *"Too stiff. That was a mistake! This is not going well!"* The piece includes a section where the left hand moves in a different rhythm from the right, a part that is tricky but gorgeous. That day, my hands shook, and I couldn't do it justice.

When I received the news that I hadn't been accepted for lessons at the Con, I wasn't surprised. But, the rejection punched a hole in my gut and made me question my playing. *"Not good enough. Unworthy. Not a pianist,"* my gremlins shouted. Until then, my love of music had been personal, not professional. I didn't care how "objectively" good I was, as long as I kept improving. But now, the verdict was in: I would never be "a real pianist." Judged, diminished, and deflated, I paid for a few months of lessons from an advanced conservatory student, then gave up and focused on my studies. I didn't touch the keys for another 12 years.

Sara wrote about how difficult it had been for her to find a cello teacher willing to take on an adult beginner. Refusing to give up, she continued her search until she found one. She began studying and practicing. Sometimes, she played recitals with children one-quarter her age. But, as Sara described her cello, her love for it was palpable. I could almost see the instrument's lustrous spruce and maple woods and hear its burnished sound.

I remember loving my piano like that.

When I moved to Seattle at 32, I attended a voice workshop in the home of a professional musician. In the middle of his living room studio sat a gorgeous grand piano, and I couldn't take my eyes off it.

A house is not a home without a piano.

Right then and there, I decided to buy my own. The following week, I found an affordable older piano in the want ads. After checking with my three roommates to make sure it was OK to move it into our group home, I bought it. I started practicing again, ecstatic to play music I'd once loved. But there was a difference from my high school days: back spasms. If I made a mistake, my back would constrict as if someone had tightened a crank. Some days, I could only play for ten minutes before I had to lie on the floor with my feet braced against the wall to ease the pain.

I was still trying to play when, at 36, I met Steve. But my newly married life, combined with work at the university and on my doctorate, made it hard to continue. By my late forties, I rarely played. My parents gave us their beautiful upright grand when they moved to a retirement center, and we brought it to the island. I occasionally played at Christmas, but for the most part, our piano sat unused. Over time, it became just another piece of furniture.

Sara finished reading her essay and received many appreciative comments, mine included. I was grateful that the dim lights obscured the tear dripping down my cheek. Sarah's love for music had opened a door for me, rendering lame my excuses for no longer playing.

My Muse, Isabel, whispered,

"Be kind, dear. Go back to your old friend and start playing again. It will remember you."

When I returned home, I rummaged through my old sheet music and found a few beginner pieces that looked simple enough. Because of the new pandemic-required lockdown, I had extra time at home to practice. Isabel had advice for me:

"Go easy. Get to know your old friend, my dear. Enjoy being together again—and start slowly. Why not pick a few simple pieces and play for just five minutes? That would be quite wonderful. And make lots of mistakes. If the spasms come, stop and rest. Then, if you like, try again."

In preparation for my first time back at the piano, I opened its lid and put my fingers on the keys. I did basic scales and warm-up exercises and was happy that my fingers, stiff and unpracticed, still recognized notes. I played a couple of beginner pieces and then began Chopin's

"Waltz in C," an easy composition. After a few minutes I had to stop, not because of my back or the difficult playing, but because tears had clouded my glasses. I was playing again—Chopin—and his simple piece sounded so beautiful. I sat on the bench stroking the piano and polishing the dust from its cabinet.

My dear friend. I'm back. Thank you for never giving up on me. I left you for so long, but I returned, and you remembered. And now, I will stay.

Singing and Silence

Let your sound begin in silence
and carry you into new realms.
—MARCO

*M*usic came rushing back into my life. As I became reacquainted with my instrument, I wondered if I might try singing as well, especially since the pandemic had prompted many teachers to offer classes online. I had not sung with anyone since my forties when I'd studied with my voice teacher, Peggy. Her approach to singing authentically without any "singerly" affectation seemed unique and, after she died, I hadn't wanted to work with anyone else. I remembered how she'd laugh with her students and tell us not to try to sing. "Just allow the voice to come forth," she'd say, "and, incidentally, you'll be singing." When I first met her, I was a struggling new MBA adrift in my career. Peggy had anchored me, and she taught me about life, spirituality and wonder, along with how to use the voice. I missed her terribly.

Many years later, during the pandemic, a friend recommended another voice teacher named Chloë Goodchild who also believed in cultivating a natural or "naked" voice. Like Peggy, she cared about *expressing* our souls rather than *impressing* others. I gulped and enrolled in Chloë's course online where I joined hundreds of people from around the world for weekly classes and practice sessions.

Chloë knew that many of her students brought pain from their vocal pasts. Many of us had been lifers in the million-member "I can't sing" club. We often could identify exactly when we learned to hide our voices, tuck our tails between our legs, constrict our larynxes and only sing when alone. I wasn't the only one to have shut down in third grade. In my case, it happened when Mrs. Johnson had humiliated me in front of the class. Almost 60 years later, I could still hear her words: *"My dear, your voice is sticking out. Remember, you are not a soloist."*

Chloë's approach blended an understanding of the voice, years of spiritual training in India, and deep compassion for those who had forgotten how natural it is to sing. She taught us to use silence before and after making a sound by offering a koan-like question, "What is the quality of the silence left after you sing?"

The truth was that I never heard silence. I had—and have—tinnitus, so there is a permanent ringing in my ears. Yet, the silence Chloë described lived underneath the ringing. It was a spiritual state—one I could enter when singing or sitting at the keyboard. Silence became the field "out beyond right and wrong," the poet Rumi once described.

Singing and silence became a growing part of my life. I sang daily to the horses. I experimented with making "ugly" nasal sounds, intoning growly baritone sounds, and allowing my voice to sound warbly and break. When I sang to my mare before a ride, she relaxed, lowered her head, licked her lips, and softened her eyes. I think she appreciated how my singing led to a more relaxed time together.

Marco supported my efforts, saying: *"In silence, you can find the mystery from which all creation appears. It offers a safe place to linger in the unknown. All sound is enhanced by silence."*

Sound Healing

Sound is seeding the joy within you
and bringing you home.
—Isabel

Chloë's classes drew many practitioners skilled in different aspects of music and sound healing. Soon, I was learning about the power of humming, chanting, drumming, tuning forks, and singing bowls. Many of the practices seemed both enjoyable and potentially healing, although I couldn't quantify their results.

I began listening to online "sound baths," during which I relaxed into the vibrations produced by singing bowls, chimes, and gongs. I sometimes felt as if I were entering a field where I was more open to invisible, spiritual forces—no theology required.

Because I was struggling with my physical energy and had become interested in brain health, I decided to explore how sound and music might add to my stamina and support my brain. I bought a specially engineered program from a company that studied music's impact on the mind. After 20 minutes each day of listening to their curated classical pieces, I felt more grounded and creative. After listening to their program of world rhythms, I felt more coordinated.

As I continued to listen to these programs and sing with Chloë, the range of my voice expanded. I could sing two or three notes higher than I had in the past. But what was more interesting was how, when

I stopped trying to sing and only vocalized—just playing around with notes, I could sing even further outside of my range. When I did, I'd occasional enter an altered state. I'd sense an energetic presence surrounded by a golden light, whom I named "Tia Sophia." Unlike the Muses, she offered no words or direct communications. She reminded me instead of a female priestess or goddess—a force perhaps known to me in a distant past. Then, I sometimes started singing unintelligible words in a kind of gibberish that seemed to come from a deep well within.

Believe me, I'd never had any connection with goddesses or energetic priestesses before—not to mention babble-like languages that seemed to spring out of nowhere. If you had said the word "goddess" to me when I was in my fifties, I would have imagined women in gauzy dresses dancing barefoot in the moonlight at midnight—not the world I inhabited. I had no frame of reference then for what I was experiencing, and I still don't. It's tempting to wonder whether I'm making all this up, just as it was once tempting to question the presence of the Muses.

Thankfully, sound can transport me to places beyond my understanding where I can observe my experience. If it opens the door to more mystery . . . well, then, so be it.

Although I was far from being a healer, prophet, or priestess in my current incarnation, I occasionally wondered if I had had such a role in a distant past—in a world far different from my feet-on-the-ground, MBA-endorsed reality. The idea of past lives was only a concept to me, not something I could verify through my experience. Yet, I occasionally wondered whether there was anything from the past that had made me so cautious about sharing my spiritual interests and intuitive sides with people who might not understand them. Maybe it was because I had run in professional circles where ideas that did not seem "realistic" or empirically proven were given little weight or even mocked. Or, was it possible that my reluctance could also be traced to a time back beyond this lifetime to the days when women healers, witches, and guides were killed for what they knew?

Twice, I'd watched Francis Poulenc's gorgeous opera *Dialogue of the Carmelites* and been deeply affected by it—beyond what I thought such a story would normally evoke in me. The historical opera is about a group of Carmelite nuns during the French Revolution who have to choose between giving up their faith and giving up their lives. During the final scene, each nun walks toward the guillotine, singing "Salve Regina" as she climbs the scaffolding to her death. At the last moment, the one holdout, a nun who has been unsure what to do, decides to stand for her faith and joins the queue. It's an edge-of-your-seat culmination to the opera and a very moving moment. Yet, for me, it was more, and I wasn't prepared for my reactions. I sobbed and sobbed, thinking, *This lives in me. I know something about this.*

Of course, my connection to women who died for their faith was not provable, nor did it need to be. The world of sound had opened a door to spaces and insights beyond the boundaries of my mind. As I continued singing with Chloë Goodchild and others, I felt carried on a soul journey into a new world—one that seemed both strange and familiar.

Playing Again

For several months after returning to the piano, I maintained a consistent practice routine. Steve professed to enjoy my playing, even with its abundance of wrong notes (again, he's a keeper), and when he cleaned the kitchen after supper, I spent time with my old friend. After my years of absence, just being at the keyboard for 25 minutes felt like a victory.

Then, the reality of life hit, and I faced challenges. When I was toning, singing, or listening to crystal bowls, I experienced a world "out beyond my mind," where I felt no worry about making mistakes. But when I played the piano, I heard the difference between right notes and wrong notes, and mistakes made me wince.

Despite my years away from the keyboard, I wasn't a beginner, even though I often played music from introductory study books. Finding my "beginner's mind" and a delightful, non-judgmental curiosity wasn't easy when I knew what was "good."

When I gardened, I didn't care about mistakes. (And yes, I killed a lot of plants.) When I wrote, words never screamed, "Wrong! Wrong!"— even when my prose felt flat. In improv class, nothing was a mistake. Yet, when I took out my old sheet music, I saw a legacy of red marks identifying the pieces I had once played. On the one hand, I loved being able to work with the music I had learned 50 and 60 years earlier. On the other, all of the correction symbols brought back memories—not all good. Even though as a 69-year-old, no one was standing by my side judging me, I still felt an internal presence reprimanding me for my mistakes. No wonder my back stiffened.

I continued practicing in the evenings until the days became longer and the high season for gardening began. Then, I took a break from regular practice, telling myself that I would start back soon. But the truth was that my "playing" had begun to feel too much like hard work, taxing a part of my brain that already felt overworked from writing and editing. I knew breaking my practice rhythm was risky, but I did it anyway.

Not surprisingly, my break stretched into months. Then, it was a year. I knew I would return to the piano eventually, since I had given it my word. But I needed to find a way to make my time with it more fun. I wanted to love notes the way I loved watercolors being poured onto the page—with childlike wonder and delight.

One day, listening to a streaming music service, I discovered the work of the contemporary Dutch composer and pianist Joep Beving. I listened to one of his piano pieces and became mesmerized, playing it again and again. Soon, I used his compositions as soundtracks for my editing. They were more than background sounds; they anchored me in a deep part of myself where words flowed more effortlessly.

Because I thought I might be able to play Beving's pieces, I asked Steve for a set of his sheet music for Christmas. Soon, I was playing the compositions that I knew so well from my hours of listening. I marveled at the progressions, savoring them like a flow of colors. His work did not require the measured precision needed for Bach.

Love was leading me. Perhaps I'd return someday to my classical music books, warm-ups, and scales. I still wanted to develop skills and help my fingers become more fluid, but first, I had to keep recovering from my fear of mistakes.

Perhaps I need more music like Beving's so I can explore the beauty of sound and relax without the need for exactness.

Marco whispered:

"Yes. It's the love. If you stay connected to it, it will carry you through the pain and hurt from past experiences. Play because you love it, and let that be why you sit down at the keys. Play because of the beauty inside the pieces that wants to break you open. When you let beauty and love propel you forward, all else will arrange itself."

Beautiful
Dark Places

Shitty News

Whitecaps danced across the waters of Puget Sound. A few sailboats braved them, enjoying gusty winds and a cerulean sky. Mount Baker gleamed on the horizon. While on some days, being tied to a ferry system meant long waits and stress, on days like this one in late spring of 2019, the 20-minute ride back to Vashon was a pinch-myself opportunity to be surrounded by the beauty of our inland sea. I scanned the surface of the water for any sight of orcas. None were out, so I decided to use my last minutes on board to check for urgent emails. *Only for a moment*, I promised myself as I scanned the subject lines.

My reverie was shattered abruptly as I read the title of an email from my sister: "Shitty news." In her brief note to our brother and me, she said that she'd been diagnosed with ovarian cancer, an aggressive, take-no-prisoners disease. I knew little about it, but I would soon learn from the grim looks on my friends' faces when I shared my news that it was a cancer to fear.

As her news hit, I collapsed on the ferry seat, gut-punched.

No! This can't be. I'm 68. She's 65. This is too soon. We were meant to grow old together.

My sister and I had experienced our share of joys, annoyances, celebrations, disagreements, collaborations, laughter, and tensions. We had grown closer during the last five years of our mother's life as we worked together to support her. Despite our differences, I admired and respected my sister enormously, and her gifts for organization and detail far exceeded mine.

She can't leave. I did not sign up for this.

The stories I had about our relationship—both past and future—were stripped bare. Yes, we might have bugged each other as kids, but did any of that matter now? I only wanted the Truth of our relationship—and the Truth was that I loved her very, very much. The only narrative I wanted for us going forward was about the sacredness of our remaining time together.

After all my years in "death training," I thought I was prepared for this. I thought I could be OK with it. But I wasn't.

Once again, my bluff had been called.

Potholes of Despair

$\mathcal{S}$uddenly, I found myself in my late sixties facing the likelihood that the two people I loved most in the world—Steve and my sister—wouldn't be around to share my final years. Even as I reveled in the joy of creating, I felt the weight of anticipatory loneliness and loss.

As he entered his early eighties, Steve had begun dealing with a laundry list of ailments, including heart problems, a lung condition, and a failed hip replacement—along with a few extras thrown in for good measure. At 86, much of this was not curable. Hip surgeons would shake their head and say, "Better to deal with hip pain than risk your life in surgery." (Steve eventually found a doctor who could replace his hip without using the general anesthesia deemed too dangerous for him.) Up until this point in life, I'd lived with the hope that he would "get better" and resume most of what he had been able to do. But by the time Steve hit his mid-eighties, I knew that he'd never go back to how he had been. I kept returning to my mantra: We must make the most of what we have.

As the number of physical activities Steve and I could do together decreased, I learned to love our simple moments more. Thinking about losing him could turn a quick pea soup lunch into a treasure or make the opportunity to sit in bed watching a movie a holy treat.

And, the reality was that my physical health was fading too. I begged doctors—allopathic, naturopathic, and chiropractic—to help me reclaim the level of energy that had once propelled me through my days. I sought opinions from specialists, learned new meditation practices, tried supplements that sounded promising, spent time outdoors, and chanted. But, despite my "healthy living" habits, it was time to accept that I, like Steve, might have to live with limits.

I continued to ride my horse, and I watched as preteen girls at my trainer's barn started lessons and surpassed me within a year. Riding had been a lifelong dream that I hadn't fulfilled until I was 42. But even though I enjoyed jumping, fear entered the picture, and small obstacles began to scare me. With my osteoporosis, I couldn't afford to fall. I looked at my beautiful mare and wondered how much time we would work together before she became a pasture pet.

Looking into the future, I saw a frontier of loss. I knew I had inner strength and could count on it to help me through my concerns about Steve's health and my sister's. Yet, there were days when sadness about the probable future got to me. While I was not, thankfully, depressed in a clinical sense, I was prone to bouts of deep melancholy where I felt like I operated at half-mast. The gremlins would dance around with messages to make life feel hopeless (*"It's no use! It's never going to work!"*) and increase my ever-present anxiety. After 30 days of dank, dark Northwest weather, doing almost anything would feel too heavy. I'd sit as if glued to the couch, meditating and searching for any little light that could get me to move.

During the pandemic and its aftermath, I felt as if the world had grown weary along with me. I used writing to navigate my path. In my weekly blog posts, I shared anything I thought could help me and others find hope and cut through brain fog. Even though I titrated how much news I took in, the headlines from an almost daily stream of tragedies could bring me to tears: another school shooting, a steady increase in global temperatures, and the brutal manifestations of racism. Maybe such ongoing awfulness had always been part of life, but, in the past, we didn't have 24/7 access to news of it. Despite my innate belief in the core goodness of people, I questioned whether I could justify my optimism when so much hate was spewing out of politicians, pundits, and social media channels.

And my sadness wasn't just about external events. I'd sometimes think about my life and worry about whether I'd achieved what I was born to do or if I should be doing more. I compared the naïve optimism I had in 1969 about changing the world, saving the planet, and ending corporate greed with the reality I saw around me. When I died, would I be leaving a planet that was basically doomed?

When things looked particularly bleak, I'd turn to meditation, chanting, or expressive arts to pull myself out. Caffeine also helped in the short term—until my energy crashed again. When things felt really bad, I turned to my most basic prayer: "*PLEASE help*." Or, I would just lie on the floor, and allow myself to be trampled with dog love as the boys smothered my face in kisses.

Because I was both self-employed and older, I was no longer receiving "atta girl!" encouragement or external reinforcements. Throughout my life, I'd been buoyed along by a good grade report, a fun date, an acceptance into college, an exciting adventure, a new job, a successful performance review, or a hoped-for consulting contract. Boosts like these could shift my mood when I felt down. But they had also led to a dependence on outside stimulation to buoy myself up.

And, the flipside of grooving on praise was being super sensitive to criticism. As much as I looked forward to publishing a book after years of effort, I worried how I would deal with the cruel comments and negative reviews that might accompany putting my work out for others to judge. I knew that creativity coaches said, "Rejecting your work isn't the same as rejecting you," but my body wasn't convinced. When a friend read some of my work and said, "No thanks, not for me," it hurt. Even a hint of rejection could trigger a shitstorm of feelings.

Isabel stepped in to help:

"Be gentle, my dear. When you publish, we'll need a little self-care plan. Just remember that your book will enable you to discover unexpected delights and beautiful connections you hadn't anticipated. And whenever you help one person, you will feel so happy."

Getting older invited—actually, it required—me to become more internally motivated. My art, in whatever form it took, needed to be about enjoying the process and weaning myself off of the obligation to create products that others liked. My path abounded in opportunities to explore that continued to feel exciting—as long as I didn't trip into potholes of despair.

This Hard Thing

*We cannot promise that the world won't be difficult and break
your heart. Yet, this is your time to be here, the only time you
have to express beauty in a way that can comfort others—or
even yourself. Return to your creative core when you need
a place of holiness and wholeness. Let it be your anchor.*
—MARCO

I lay in bed rocking myself on the morning of November 8th, 2016, after the results of the U.S. presidential elections were announced. Fearing the outcome, I had barely slept. I had wanted a woman president who would be a voice for compassion and civility. Instead, the doors had been thrown open to misogyny, lies, and hate.

Curled into a fetal ball, I let myself be comforted by a soft blanket of depression. Eventually, I got up to feed the animals. I cut myself a deal: I would stand, move slowly, and head toward the kitchen. I only planned a few steps ahead: *Go to the stove. Put on the kettle. Make tea. Go to the paddock.*

I doubted my friends were rising quickly. They'd probably hunkered down with their feelings of grief, numbness, and anger as well. Only a few weeks before, we'd practically toasted an almost certain victory for women— the one for which we had waited decades. That dream had evaporated.

My hands shook as I drank my tea and then put on old clothes to go outside. The horses welcomed me with gentle nuzzles, oblivious to what had just happened to the country. I thanked them for that. I finished my equine chores and remembered it was Wednesday—blog-writing day. If I planned to publish on Thursday, according to my typical schedule, I would need to start writing.

If I can find a way to deal with my grief, perhaps I can help my readers.

I walked to the cabin, hoping to find sanctuary within its welcoming walls. I sank into my writing chair, pulled out my computer, and stared into space until Isabel appeared. *"Be kind, dear, and have no expectations of yourself—especially today. Why don't you take some time to search online for something that could bring you comfort?"*

I nodded and began to surf the internet. On the late John O'Donohue's website, I found a description of how traditional Irish farmers, travelling on a marshy, barely navigable road, would throw down a "ciseach" of sticks and rushes. With this temporary patch in place, donkeys and carts could pass. In times of grief, a ciseach could help us travel to more solid ground.

Writing my blog will be my ciseach today.

I also discovered inspiration on the website of Parker Palmer, an educator whom I greatly admired. There, his teaching partner, singer-songwriter Carrie Newcomer, had posted a video of her song "You Can Do This Hard Thing." Her beautiful voice and storytelling wisdom felt like a balm. I sensed that she knew something about the pain many of us were feeling. Her narrator faces tragedy—"the worst"—and does not want to be alone. She phones someone she loves and finds comfort—the solace many of us might be needing. As I listened, immersed in her song, the floodgate that had held back the sobs within me broke. Hearing her words helped me to realize that I wasn't yet numb. The defeat hurt. It was right to cry. I let tears cover my cheeks and drench my shirt as I played her video again and again. Then, after 30 minutes of weeping, I felt whole. I could write. I shared with my readers the idea of using a ciseach to get through hard times.

Within an hour, I had drafted a post and reclaimed a sense of my agency. Misogyny would not triumph—not if those who cared deeply about justice in the world kept expressing themselves and creating.

Goodbye to a Muse

By the time I was wrapping up this book, Isabel and I were no longer meeting regularly. Instead of visiting over tea, she was more likely to whisper a comment or two when I was out walking. One morning, as I was taking a stroll, she announced:

"My dear, I am fading. Don't be concerned, for this isn't a bad thing; it is natural and good. But it means I won't be around much. I need to spend time resting. I am fine, but I am changing. Please know that I love you, that we will always be connected, and that I will try to be there if you need me. Trust that you have much support beyond what you know."

I didn't get it. If Isabel only lived in my imagination (still a possibility), why would she go away? My eyes welled up. I didn't care who she was or what she was; I loved her grandmotherly support, presence, and wit and was unsure what life would look like without it. I wished I could sit by her side and offer my comfort—although I knew that she was fine, and I was the one who was hurting.

Isabel had opened the door to the world of Muses. She had taken me deeper into my intuition and ways of knowing, and she had guided me beyond my old beliefs. She'd invited me to trust and loosened the grip of the self-judgment that often surfaced through my gremlins. The prospect of losing the comfort of our chats in the cabin when I had sat, tea at my side, and typed her words was heartbreaking.

Yet, I sensed she was right; she needed to move on, as did I. Marco had emerged, and I was discovering different ways of sensing the imaginal through meditation, prayer, art, and sound. On my walks, I would think of the subtle worlds and ask for help "in case you are there." I offered gratitude for the support I might not yet recognize. I sensed that I was not alone.

Do Muses age and eventually pass? Or did Isabel receive another assignment?

I had no idea. Isabel added:

"Your job, my dear, is to stay out of despair and keep turning toward the light. We are all in this together. Welcome the presences and energies who want to help. Know that more will follow. Be grateful—as you are. And, then, delight in each small step. Follow the light, and share what you discover. Let that be your path right now. I love you and will miss our cups of tea and your silly dogs. Please hug them for me."

As I typed these words for this book, Royce unexpectedly abandoned his post under my desk, jumped up, and attempted to climb—all 60 pounds of him—into my computer chair. He wouldn't stop kissing my face until I spoke about how much Isabel meant to us both. After telling him that she would live on in our hearts and explaining how grateful I was for that, he finally jumped down and resumed his place on the floor.

I pictured Isabel smiling, wherever she was.

Gratitude

My creative work became even more important to me as I looked at sustaining myself through darkness in the years ahead.

My friend Rita, a former nun 18 years my senior, inspired me to walk this path. She had published two books in her seventies, and a third in her eighties, and she showed me how one could endure severe hardship and keep going. As members of the same women's group, we'd enjoyed long conversations on the retreats we'd attended over the years. I loved the moments we had spent talking poetry under the shade of a tall Douglas fir tree while watching the does wandering around the grounds. Rita was and is a deeply spiritual woman who exudes caring and has an outrageous sense of humor.

But her deep faith didn't spare her from a "dark night of the soul" when a medication blunder broke her back and almost broke her spirit. During her months in a nursing home, the acute pain she experienced tested her in ways she could have never imagined. She later told me, "I lost my will to live. It was only the faith of my family and friends that pulled me through. They believed in me when I could no longer believe in myself. I saw myself mirrored in their eyes."

I was part of this group of women. We had rallied around and prayed for Rita daily. We fed her back our vision of who she was when she couldn't see it. Feeling the love and support, she pulled herself out of the depths.

When she was finally able to return to her condo, she continued her morning ritual expressing gratefulness for her many blessings: She would step onto her balcony, look across the waters of Puget Sound toward the mountains, lift her arms, and pray, "Thank you for this day. Thank you for my life. Thank you for ___" —filling in the phrase with what was good about her life.

I borrowed her gesture. In a five-minute walk to feed the horses, I blessed the madrona, blueberries, dandelions, and flies. I blessed the stinging nettles that I usually hated, admiring the dense root systems that allowed them to persevere despite my attempts at their eradication. I blessed the friends in my life and the angels, nature spirits, elemental beings, and faeries—any benevolent spirits that happened to be around.

I wasn't able to bless my sister's cancer—not yet, even though I saw great strength emerging in her as she dealt with her condition. But I took heart from the words of the Benedictine monk, David Steindl-Rast, a lifelong student of gratitude. He said that we don't have to be grateful for everything, but in everything, we could find something for which to be thankful.

In meditation, a phrase came to me:

Today. This Day. Right Now.

I raised my arms for this day, for my sister, for Steve, and for the gift of this life. There would always be something for which I could give thanks.

Friends in Fair and Foul Weather

When I asked myself the question, *How would I survive if the worst happened?* I, like Rita, thought about my friends.

I had discovered late in life that, despite my love of teaching and speaking in public, I was an introvert. I preferred a few intimate friendships to gobs of casual friends. I was happy working alone if I was doing something creative—even pulling weeds. Yet, I knew that part of what allowed me to sustain so much aloneness was having a network of kindred spirits in my life.

One of my most creative friendships was (and is) with Lori, a fellow misfit from business school who became a pillar of support on my post-midlife journey. When we reconnected in our sixties, we discovered a common passion for living more creative lives. We shared our respective callings and rallied each other with weekly check-ins. We became mutual advocates for following an artful path—wherever that might take us. Like trained mountaineers, we anticipated the dangers on the journey ahead and could anchor each other if one of us got lost in a storm of self-doubt or self-judgment. When I told Lori, "Getting published is a pipe dream," or, "My writing sucks," she reminded me of how far I had come. When she told me, "I haven't done anything creative this week," I reminded her of the art and skill she put into caring for her mom and editing her mother's personal history. We could whine to each other freely, then shift gears and plot a way forward.

When the pandemic cut off social activities on our island, I found colleagues from around the world who shared my passions. As I sang weekly with new friends online, my voice became more confident. My "virtual writing pod," a four-woman group created prior to the pandemic, supported each other to keep going despite deaths, housing challenges, and writing rejections. We seized opportunities to celebrate small breakthroughs.

These friends became part of a special group I secretly called my "foul weather friends," or "FWFs"—a term I borrowed from two Vietnam War-era folksingers, Steve Addiss and Bill Crofut. They used it to describe their friendship with Pete Seeger. Given Seeger's fame, commitments, and touring schedule, Addiss and Crofut knew they would rarely meet up with him face-to-face. Yet they knew Pete would always be there for them if the weather turned nasty. My FWFs qualified for their special status by facing their own tragedies, losses, illnesses, and deaths. In stormy seas, they were the ones who could be trusted to toss a ring buoy or a life preserver without offering platitudes, homilies, false cheer, or suggestions to "buck up."

The older I grew, the more precious such friends became.

Viva Italia

Passing through Purgatory

Life may not work the way you want,
but if you hang in there, it usually works out.
—Isabel

"We found a tumor in your bladder. We think it's cancerous. But, hopefully, we can cut it out."

This news was yet another blow to a deteriorating 86-year-old body. Steve took it bravely, despite knowing that the diagnosis effectively aborted our plans to travel together to Italy that July. Since international travel had looked possible in 2022, we'd spent the end of 2021 charting a five-week trip. I was to spend the first half of it painting with Dana Lynne Andersen at her studio near Assisi. Steve was supposed to join me afterwards for a jaunt through Tuscany. His surgery was scheduled for the week before I was to leave, preempting that plan.

That left me in a quandary.

Should I stay or should I go?

Steve was adamant that I go. "You've waited two years to study with Dana, and you told me this would be the trip of a lifetime. Now, you can use all five weeks to work with her at her studio. I'll miss you, but the animals will be happy to have me home." Our dog, Winston, seemed to agree as he backed his butt up to Steve for a rub.

I protested. "I can't leave you here hurting."

"It's not going to be like that. My doc says the recovery should be straightforward, and I won't need special care. Plus, I've got plenty of friends who have offered to help. And what about all those weeks you've spent trying to learn Italian?"

Not so successfully. I used to love learning languages, but now the verbs enter my brain and tumble out the other side.

Steve was right, though. I needed to go. The trip felt like the culmination of a journey that had begun 15 years earlier when the message *peonies* directed me toward pleasure, beauty, and creative expression— all of which I hoped to immerse myself in during this trip. It felt like a reward for staying steadfast in my commitment to creating, despite numerous doubts and gremlin attacks.

Still, I was a stress-mess during the two weeks leading up to Steve's surgery. Even though his doctors were confident, hearing "the c-word" made me shudder. After all his heart problems, I never thought we'd have to deal with this one, too. I walked around our house jittery, unable to focus on my writing or much of anything. I had to give myself little directives to manage my days: *Feed the horses. Write the check. Do the wash.*

But when the day came for his surgery, I felt strangely calm. I surprised myself with a new learning: *Sometimes anticipating an event is tougher than experiencing it.*

It helped that the day was balmy and clear when I dropped Steve off at 7 am. I headed out for a latte and a long walk, anticipating that the operation would only take a couple of hours. Fortunately, the surgeon called me right on schedule with good news and an invitation to join Steve in the recovery room.

I walked into a maze of low lights, beeping sounds, and curtained "rooms." Then I saw his beamy smile greeting me and brightening the space—a pure Steve welcome. The doctor at his bedside was also smiling. "We were lucky. The tumor hadn't spread, and we took it all out. Steve can go home tomorrow, and we'll have the biopsy results within the week." I breathed a full-body sigh of relief. *We made it through this one.*

Seven days later, Steve drove me to the airport, lingering for one last hug in the terminal before heading off to an appointment with his oncologist. I walked to the gate, foregoing the shops and eateries to conserve my depleted energy for the overnight flight to Rome via Frankfurt. In the air, I read simple stories in Italian and fantasized about the twice-baked croissants awaiting me in Rome. When the flight attendant offered me a bland, cheesy-something dinner, I declined—a mistake I would later regret.

I had thought of my trip to Italy as a visit to paradise. What I didn't realize was that I'd have to make a pit stop in purgatory first. I arrived at the baggage claim area in Rome dizzy from lack of sleep and waited as the bags went round and round. When the carousel stopped spinning, I awoke from my stupor to realize that my suitcase hadn't arrived. I headed off to find the lost baggage window. By the time I reached it, 40 other people from my flight had lined up ahead of me. I counted the minutes that the lone clerk was taking to process each passenger's paperwork—about 15. By my calculations, I had a five-hour wait ahead of me. Unfortunately, I was right.

As I settled into my place on the concrete floor, I received a text from Steve. His biopsy had revealed a very aggressive bladder cancer, which, although it had not metastasized, needed to be treated preventatively with a prolonged course of immunotherapy. Not surprisingly, he felt scared, demoralized, and lonely.

Exhausted, thirsty, and famished, I wanted to scream.

Shit! Shit! Shit! It's too much! I can't take it all: the bad news, Steve's pain, and now this horrible baggage mess. I can't stand this—I'm going to collapse. I can't wait five hours, and I WON'T stay here. My husband has cancer. I shouldn't have to wait in line.

I knew that my agitation—as well as my sense of entitlement—was off the charts. This was still the trip of a lifetime, an enormous privilege, and a gift from Steve and the gods. But I was used to things working, and my head was spinning from a lack of food. I continued ranting until Isabel returned for a special visit to help me off my hysterical cliff.

"You can't do anything, darling, so be with what is. It will get better, I promise."

I sighed, got out a sweater to cushion my butt, and leaned against my daypack. My fellow passengers joked about the absurdity of our situation and the broken Italian bureaucracy. The 15 of us at the back of the line became road comrades as we shared nuts, fruit, and energy bars. We held spots for each other in line so we could escape to go to the bathroom. When my phone died, a woman handed me her portable charger.

Finally, my turn at the window came. But, when I approached the clerk, I couldn't find my bag claim check. I dug deep in my purse, dumping the contents on the floor as I tried to find the stub. My gremlins had a heyday: *"How could you possibly be that stupid . . . after all that time waiting?"*

I tried to use my phone to retrieve the bag number from the airline's website, but when I looked at it, I saw "no internet connection." The clerk flashed me a "no-empathy-here" look as my face flushed. I was now the one holding up the line. Finally, the internet connection returned, and I gave the clerk my claim number. A moment later, I heard my phone ping with a text message telling me my bag was arriving from Frankfurt on carousel 32.

I raced to the ramp where I found my pod of travelers doing their happy dances as the bags tumbled down the ramp, mine included. We high-fived, celebrating our impending release from baggage purgatory. Outside the airport, I met the Italian driver I'd hired to take me to Umbria. Miraculously, he'd waited for me, though he wasn't happy about the hours he'd spent baking in his car. (Yes, he got a big tip!)

Within minutes of leaving the airport, I saw my first Italian hay field, glowing like an impressionist painting as the late afternoon sun slid across freshly mowed bales. Fields of sunflowers bowed their heads to honor the close of day. After an hour, we entered the province of Umbria and drove past historic Spoleto, where the illumined walls of the ancient stone buildings shone against the dusk's growing darkness. Two hours into the trip, I caught my first sight of the purple-gray rolling hills of Assisi. I felt them welcoming me to the land of Saint Francis and Saint Claire—and my paradise for the next month.

As tough as they were, the first 36 hours of my trip taught me a couple lessons. One: I was resilient and could rise above my inner whiner. Two: Life in Italy (or anywhere) was unlikely to go as planned. I knew this, of course. But sometimes, we need to be reminded of these profound truths—or we need to hear them differently.

Although Isabel and I were no longer meeting regularly, her presence in the airport had been like warm arms comforting me when I was shaky. Before she receded again, she reminded me,

"Life may not work the way you want, but hang in there because it usually works out."

Imaginings

Trust the essence of what you know
and be an artist of the soul.
—Marco

When I told friends that I would be "studying art in Italy," they assumed I'd be taking painting or drawing lessons and learning technique. But the Transformational Arts program at Dana's studio wasn't anything like that. I was still hesitant about making art, given my non-existent technique and minimal skills, but, for Dana's process, this was a non-issue. Our group of ten would be learning to trust our intuition and inner flow as we created. The product of our endeavors would be incidental, so painting prowess was not required. We used chanting, dancing, and meditating to open up our bodies and imaginations before we moved into making art in whatever medium spoke to us. This could be clay, collage, pastels, or tempera paints. The goal was to allow Spirit to flow through into whatever we made.

The first day of our week-long class on "Spirit, Art, and Nature" was held in the woods, in a studio set up under the shade of tall trees. As we convened Monday morning for an hour of singing and sharing, my body screamed, "I'm too tired. I don't want to do anything. I want to lie down." Very soon, I got my wish. Dana gave us our week's assignment: "Pick a spot in the woods, and create an art installation to be shared through a ritual you'll design and offer on Friday." I grabbed a blanket and headed into the forest. Within minutes, I had plunked down on a carpet of grass and collapsed. I spent the morning in my chosen spot watching the clouds dance behind the tall birch trees. A caravan of ants marched near me as I lay on my back; occasionally a straggler traversed his way across my hand. The air smelled of musky bark, decaying leaves, and the sweet freshness of new grass.

In my dreamy, jet-lagged state, I imagined the forest full of nature spirits, faeries, and Sidhe (pronounced "shee"), supernatural beings known to the ancient Celts but invisible to most of us. I'd heard them called "the people of peace" and "cousins of humanity," and I'd been told that some of them wanted to reestablish the connection with humans that they'd had lost many years ago. They, too, were concerned with the state of the planet. Of course, I didn't know any of that from my personal experience. It seemed a bit far out, but I trusted the people I knew who had met a Sidhe, and I liked the idea of including them in my project.

As I lay on the ground with a mind too tired to think or analyze, my imagination felt free to play with ideas. *What if there are Sidhe? Why not honor them here in the forest, just in case they do exist and want to connect?*

I decided that, for my installation, I'd create a "Sanctuary for the Sidhe" and invite members of that ancient people to visit. As I stood up to leave my site that morning, I saw the woods around me with fresh eyes. I saw lots of natural materials I could use, like sticks, roots, moss, rocks and feathers. On the second day, while roaming the woods, I uncovered a 20-foot-long, almost one-inch-wide morning glory vine. I dragged it to my site and tied it around a clump of trees to mark the boundaries of the space. After that, I worked each morning in class to shape a clay sculpture that would blend with the palette of forest colors I had chosen: browns, grays, beiges, greens, and blacks.

On the fourth day, I was about to celebrate the completion of my work when I heard a distinctive voice say: *"We'd like more color, please, and some glitter."* Glitter? That was completely outside of my design—and my usual style, for that matter. Could a Sidhe have made that request? I'd read that they were a colorful folk, so it wouldn't be out of character.

If they want glitter and color, I'd better give it to them.

I went back to the studio and cut shapes out of brightly-colored construction papers. I assembled pink, blue, and magenta tempera paints as well as glitter and glue to take to the woods. At my site, I brushed color onto the vines and rocks, and then I sprinkled gold, silver, and red glitter onto the paint before it dried. I decorated my cut papers and tied them to the trees and vines where they dangled like mobiles in the wind. These additions brought my site alive with an energy I had not predicted. Perhaps the Sidhe *had* spoken.

I fretted before our Friday completion ceremony; designing rituals was not my forte. How should I speak about the Sidhe when I wasn't entirely sure what they were? I took a long walk that morning, mulling over what I might say, not wanting to pretend to know more than I did. A Muse-like voice—or perhaps one of the Sidhe—intervened.

"You know more about this than you think that you know."

I was certain this was true. My walk became more confident as I strode across the crunchy birch leaves. I told myself:

Stay with the truth of your experience, open your heart, allow your imagination to guide you, and don't worry about what others will think.

After I welcomed the group to my site, I began with a legend from the days in Ireland when both Sidhe and humans knew of each other's presence. I didn't try to convince anyone of their existence; I was simply offering a tale and introducing a possibility. *"If this ancient people existed and wanted to team up with humanity to help the Earth, don't they deserve a thank-you?"* I invited my classmates to offer their gratitude and blessing for the Sidhe, and, remarkably, everyone did.

That morning, I felt like I crossed a threshold. I stepped out of an old part of myself and into a vulnerable place where I could share my intuitions about the "unseen worlds." Over the years, I had gradually been allowing more space for this kind of knowledge, but I had a hard time letting go of the idea that I might be judged for relying upon it. Through my sanctuary project, however, I had spoken from my heart and imagination, truly unshackled from the need to be "credible." My desire to honor the Sidhe had been stronger than my worries about peoples' reactions.

As I stood with the group at the close of the ritual, tingles ran up my spine, and tears hid in the corner of my eyes. Truth was, I *did* believe in the Sidhe, and I felt called to honor whatever invisible forces, spirits, or beings in the natural world wanted to help save our endangered planet.

That afternoon, after our ceremony, when I went to play in Dana's lofty indoor studio, I looked with curiosity at the blank piece of paper, ready to trust whatever was about to come through.

With Francis in the Basilica

I know Saint Francis will be there for me.
—Joaquim Kreutz

"*I* know Saint Francis will be there for me when my time comes."
Joachim Kreutz wasn't Catholic, so I wondered how he was so sure about this. I'd met my new German friend at the farm guesthouse where I was staying during my visit to Italy. Our rooms shared a terrace, and we exchanged pleasantries as we sipped our rich Italian coffees and enjoyed a view of the hills. As we talked, I discovered that he and his lovely wife, Hildegard, had worked with German Waldorf schools. My ears perked up. I had been on the board of Seattle's Waldorf school and had studied the ideas of Rudolf Steiner, whose philosophy is foundational to these innovative and creative institutions.

Steiner's work had helped me in my twenties, when I was alone and wondering *Is this all there is?* Through a fluke of circumstance, I had reconnected with a childhood friend—a Waldorf schoolteacher—who introduced me to anthroposophy, the movement inspired by Steiner's work. Although a bit skeptical at first, I became fascinated to learn how what Steiner called "knowledge of the higher worlds" was being applied to initiatives in education, religion, science, medicine, agriculture, and art. Steiner emphasized the importance of both imagination and intuition. Through the imagination, he said, we can see into a future that is not yet visible. Through our intuition, we can sense the presence of and guidance from spiritual forces.

I wondered how Steiner's ideas informed Joachim's relationship to his art. One morning, after sharing some ripe yellow plums picked from a nearby tree, I asked him. He explained that he used sculpture to help bereaved parents deal with the loss of their children. "So often, they want to hold on to the spirit of their child. But this holding hurts the child who needs to move on in the afterlife. I help the parents put their grief into the stone or piece of clay. They create something beautiful that reminds them of their love for those who have passed while allowing themselves and their departed ones to continue their spiritual journeys."

I listened to the sculptor, fascinated, noticing that I was becoming tear as currents of energy flood my chest. The coffee cup I was holding felt weightier. My Longing was telling me to listen. What Joachim was sharing was significant for me.

I was grateful when Marco stepped in to translate what I was sensing into a stream of words.

"Joachim is giving you a clue you've been seeking—an explanation of why you're drawn to transformational art. Your connection with art is not about becoming a great artist, selling products, or even expressing feelings, although you may indeed create work that pleases you and others.

"Art, for you, is about soul work—a process as well as a result. It's a way for you to celebrate beauty and mystery in a world that needs both.

"What you seek to share is a portal through which people can discover—with their own eyes and hands—a deeper sense of who they are—both in this world and in their connection to a spiritual world.

"Trust what you know. Human beings cannot save the planet alone—not anymore. We must work together with the spiritual worlds and non-physical friends like the Sidhe, who are here to help.

"Know that each time you sit down to create with an open heart, you send a healing energy into the world, even if all you do is sit at your table and paint. Trust, and become an artist of the soul. You are here to bridge worlds and to serve the Light and Love at the core of all."

I let Marco's words roll around in my mind before returning to the conversation with Joachim. Finally, I said, "I feel like Saint Francis and Saint Clair are still walking these hills."

Joachim nodded. "They are." He paused and looked out at the gentle contours of the Umbrian hills basking in the golden morning light. Then he turned back to me. "You know, I have brain cancer."

I was stunned. I had no clue; he looked so vital. But, as I compared the face I saw before me with the one on his promotional brochure, I saw a change.

"I've managed to live for two years with it and am doing well, but I may not have that much longer." He seemed remarkably calm. "But I'm not worried. A couple of months ago, Francis came to me in a dream. I'm not Catholic, but I have no doubt it was him. We have a relationship. He told me not to be afraid and promised he'd be there for me when my time came. I felt his love surround me. Now I feel at peace with dying."

I was happy for him, even as I envied his certainty. I regretted having to end the conversation when a car honked for me. I thanked him for our time together, then joined the friend who had offered to take me to Assisi.

After reaching the outskirts of the city, we parked and began a long walk through town to the Basilica that houses the tomb of Saint Francis. As we headed down the main street, we passed dozens of stores with Francis memorabilia and tchotchkes ranging from night lights and paintings to bracelets, posters, and olive oil. Tourists swarmed the sidewalks, while, at the same time, monks in long brown robes, sandals, and string belts continued their slow pilgrimages toward the large church.

There, guards stood at the door, offering simple blue satin shawls to those wanting to enter the sanctuary with bare shoulders and exposed midriffs. Religious visitors walked in quietly, genuflected, and passed into the church's enormous Upper Basilica where many settled into the hard wooden pews.

My friend wanted to visit a different corner of the church, so we separated. I headed to the Lower Basilica, one floor above the tomb of Saint Francis. Dim light protected the famous Giotto paintings that covered the ceiling. I had hardly looked at the art before three words almost knocked me off my feet: *"Pray for her."*

I gripped the pew and sat down. My heart pounded as a prayer swept through me:

Saint Francis. Be with her. Love her.

I prayed with single focus, allowing my heart to open to Francis. It didn't matter that I'd never had a personal relationship with him. I imagined his love for God and all of God's creatures. I asked him to be with my sister through her pain. She'd lived with cancer for three tough years by this point, and I had no idea how much time she'd have left. I begged Francis to hold her through all the fears, unknowns, and challenges she might face at the end of her life. Of course, if he could produce a miracle and cure her body, I would love that, too. But what I wanted most was his care for her soul.

I know, Francis, that cancer may take her body. But please, stay with her, and hold her spirit. And, when the time comes, please carry her Home.

As I prayed, my love for my sister and Saint Francis kept expanding. I was still sitting on the hard pew, and yet I had entered another field beyond the limits of the chapel. In that space, the three of us sat together, acknowledging the pain and suffering that often came with being human. At the same time, we were present to a larger wordless reality, where everything, if difficult in the moment, was going to be all right.

Francis, I can't know what lies ahead or how difficult it may be. Please share your strength with us and your love.

I sat quietly in the pew, trying to drink in a sense of deep peace so I could call upon it when I was back home with my sister. I trusted—and trust—that when I lose her or Steve, Francis will be there—for all of us.

A Simpler Path

Remember you are whole and have always been.
We are not here to be perfect.
—Marco

I occasionally wondered, as I reveled in my Umbrian paradise, whether experiencing so much delight was fair when my sister and Steve were suffering. Marco offered strongly worded advice on this topic:

> *"Feeding your soul and spirit with joy will allow you to give more. Replenish yourself and learn what fills you—and enables you to help over the long haul."*

Being in Italy without Steve changed the nature of my trip. I chose not to rent a car and depended on friends and drivers to take me to buy groceries. Touring the area sounded complicated. Plus, the heat was sweltering, with temperatures hitting 95 degrees or more in the cities. So, instead of joining the throngs visiting Florence, Rome, or Venice, I stayed where I was, enjoying the hilltop breeze in the small commune of Catecuccio where the guesthouse sat. Yes, I missed seeing the work of Michelangelo, but I treasured every sunset, morning walk, and blissful dip in the pool. "Slow and simple" became my mantra for the month.

Each morning, I went for a walk at dawn, made an espresso, ate a simple breakfast, and then headed off to the studio on an old rented bicycle with a big basket in front. At the studio, we chanted, danced, made art, and worked through the morning. Class ended at 1:30 pm, when I usually returned to the guesthouse for a quick swim and a light lunch. I could edit my book in the afternoon or return to the studio. I pinched myself in gratitude for my good fortune as I savored the easy rhythm of my days.

With each passing week, I better understood the nature of transformative art. For me, it came out of an intuitive connection—a listening. It required responding to whatever was present in the moment and taking a journey with the imagination. Through a daily process, I could connect with higher energies and find joy. I could feed my soul and work with complicated feelings without needing to analyze them.

Despite my mostly blissful life in Italy, a change in plans, a logistics snafu, or a turbulent sleep could still whack me out. One morning, I was feeling particularly ornery when I arrived in class. We began by chanting as we convened, but even the sound of the harmonium didn't lift my spirits. I participated in our meditation but decided not to do the morning's assignment until I had done some inner reckoning.

I left the studio and sat in the rocky soil behind the back door, wrestling with an onslaught of angry thoughts. Despite the joy I felt most days in Italy, I had tripped, once again, on my own expectations and was having trouble pulling myself out of the pit. As I stared out at the garden and distant horizon, I saw a setting that was soft and soothing, with lavender and pink roses, olive groves, and blue-tinged hills. But inside of me, all I could find was blackness.

I made myself a deal: I would go back inside, but I would only work with colors that called to me. In the studio, I gathered black pastels and took my spot at a table in front of a 2' x 2' sheet of paper. I let myself flow into the process, swaying as I placed dark arcs on the page. Then, I filled the space under the curves with tight angular marks until a sea of black emerged. I didn't think about where I was going or the result until 20 minutes into the process, when I stepped back from the table and looked at my work. I then felt called to grab a deep purple pastel and continue coloring. Before long, I added blue and silver—and I noticed that I was no longer feeling so dark inside.

After an hour, I was almost done, but the work called for one more touch. Little scraps of silver foam had been left on the table, and I decided to use them to frame what had emerged as a circular mandala-like form.

In working on my piece, my angry mood had melted and been replaced by curiosity. I enjoyed the boldness I saw in front of me. I wasn't sure what it represented, but I was pleased that I'd made something. After a lunch break, I returned to the studio to do the morning's assignment: a visioning collage. Black still spoke to me, so I glued scraps of black construction paper on a 2' x 4' background. A message came through me, which I transcribed onto one of the black sections with a silver pen. It said, "Don't fear your fear."

I reflected for a moment and recognized how underneath so much of the anxiety, anger, and occasional depression I felt, there was a fear that felt deeply held and primal. Did it come from my toddler days, from which I carried few specific memories? Or did I inherit it from my mother, whom I suspected carried more pain from her youth than she ever spoke about? Did my fear come from another lifetime, as I imagined when I watched *Dialogue of the Carmelites?* I didn't need to know. Perhaps I couldn't know.

What I could do was stop hiding the part of myself where that fear lived. It was time to stop shaming the little girl who had carried it, hiding her away so I could be perceived as strong and worthy. I doubt the hiding had ever worked, since people usually sense what you are feeling underneath what you try to present. But as I had discovered with the little girl in madras and my young rejected dancer, parts of me needed more understanding, love, and opportunities to play. Would my fearful self enjoy colors? Special music, art, or flowers? Better to offer her what might fill her heart rather than continue to tell her to "get over" her difficult feelings.

"Don't fear who you are," Marco whispered, *"and let even the painful feelings take you where you need to go. Remember, you are whole and have always been. We are not here to be perfect."*

The rest of my collage flowed effortlessly. I'd found my flow by allowing my darkness to come forward. I felt like I had tasted the power within transformative arts—and it was much richer and deeper than I had imagined at the start of my work in Italy. I decided to continue in Dana's certification program and embark on a year of guided independent study to become one of her "Transformative Arts Facilitators"—a big step for someone who still doubted her competency in creating visual arts. Yet, the work was a doorway into a world I felt passionate about exploring.

When the time came to leave Italy, Dana asked me how I would sustain the practices that had allowed me to find flow and connect with Spirit in the studio,

I made a list of what might help me. Gratitude topped it, followed by walking, since I had found that my long meanders in the hills calmed and centered me. Enjoying music through chanting, singing, playing the piano, and listening to sound baths felt important, as did dancing and anything else that kept me moving. I added touch and relaxation to the list, knowing how much I enjoyed playing with the animals and cuddling with Steve. I would also need to rest and sleep enough. Creating this list fortified me to return to the challenges awaiting me.

On my last day in Italy, I walked once more in the hills, thanking them along with the birds I had listened to, the pool where I had swum, the bicycle I had ridden, and the Muses I had communed with. I said goodbye to the Sidhe, my classmates, and my landlady. I took one last sip of inspiration, letting the "notes" of sorrow and sweetness blend.

The real work—staying connected, finding joy, and creating outside of the retreat setting—was about to begin.

Perfectly
Imperfect

My Father's Last Message

My father and I never talked about faith—until one day, we did. I was 46, and he was 82.

Dad was recovering from exploratory diagnostic surgery to identify the source of his persistent abdominal pain. Steve and I visited him in the hospital late in the afternoon, following an all-day singing workshop we had attended. On our way there, my mother had phoned us with the results of the procedure: Dad had non-Hodgkin's lymphoma.

The Seattle skies were thick with dark rain as we walked into his room. Dad lay immersed in shadows but gradually lifted himself as he heard our voices. The anesthesia had left him fuzzy, and he had not yet heard the news. On some level, I think he knew.

"Hi there," he said, obviously groggy from painkillers. Steve sat down on a plastic visitor's chair while I sat on a hospital stool, and we told him about our workshop. Dad continued to wake up as the light through the window continued to dim. Sitting with him at dusk felt like a kind of communion, a holy space.

When I was growing up, Dad had been my judge. His voice was embedded in my brain, always saying, *"If you can't do it right, don't do it at all."* His words fed my intense self-judgment, and we hurt each other when we fought and could not connect. But that had been 30-plus years earlier. The Dad lying before me in the hospital bed with tired blue eyes was my supporter, not my judge.

My parents had moved to the Seattle area in 1985 when I was 35, giving our family a second chance to come together as adults, complete with spouses and grandchildren. We almost lost Dad ten years later when he had a major heart attack. That day, I spent three hours in a windowless waiting room at a Seattle hospital, praying the most fervent prayer of my life: *Let him live.* He did—and that gave us three more happy years together as a family before his cancer diagnosis. During that time, he seemed more relaxed and able to share his love for all of us. The critic in him had softened and mostly disappeared.

In the crepuscular light, Dad spoke in a voice different from any I'd heard him use. "You two have faith, but I've always been a seeker."

I wanted to say, *"Dad, I'm also a seeker,"* but I held my tongue.

During our early years as a family, Dad had belonged to various Protestant churches, which I suspected he attended to support my mother or sing in the choir. In their later years, Mom and Dad attended church retreats, and he became interested in the new historical findings about Jesus. But Dad's faith had always seemed cerebral; he was as far from being a mystic as I could imagine.

He continued. "After my heart attack, I had one of those—I think you call them 'near-death experiences.'"

The air in the room stilled.

"I never told anyone. I knew I was going Home and leaving this Earth. I saw a Light, and I knew that everything was OK. It was very peaceful, very beautiful, and I wanted to keep going toward that Light. But then, I thought about your mother and how she didn't know how to use Quicken."

I almost laughed. Only my dad would return to Earth to help Mom use bookkeeping software. Whatever the reason, I was so grateful that he chose to come back.

He paused, then started again. "But I learned one thing when I was in that place: It's all about the love and the relationships." After a raspy breath, he repeated, "It's all about the love and the relationships." Then he looked me in the eye and added, "It's the only thing that matters."

I sat stunned, my body quivering. My linear, rational father would never invent a story about a spiritual experience he hadn't had. This revelation felt like a pearl I could hold on to after he was gone.

My Longing stirred within me assuring me that I was in the presence of Truth.

My father would not lie. The Light is real.

Dad never spoke again of his near-death experience. But, with reflection, I could see how it changed him. After his heart attack, he became calmer, more expressively loving, and more focused on family. The Dad I had wanted as a child emerged.

I wish I could say that his words freed me of all fear of Death, but I'm not there yet. But I keep the pearl stored in my heart. When I'm afraid of what is to come, I can slowly rub it. Its opalescent sheen reflects the light; its luster reminds me to look to beauty for sustenance.

"You Are So Lucky."

*I*n contrast to my dad, my mother offered no epiphanies during the two and a half years following her stroke. As dementia stripped her of words, her only communication was an occasional smile or blink.

However, four days after her death, I received a surprise message from a colleague with whom I hadn't spoken in four years. It read, "My heart feels for you. Your mother visited me in the last couple of days, and she has a message for you, if it's OK to share?"

I had not told this friend about my mother's death. I knew from past work together that he was an energy healer as well as a driven entrepreneur, but I had no idea that he received messages from the dead.

OK. Why not? I was open to such things—much more so of late. I texted back, "Of course. Thank you."

He replied, "It's common when people transition that their soul sticks around for a while and has messages for those they love. Her message was: 'Did I ever tell you how lucky you are?' It's on the cover of a Dr. Seuss book I had sitting on my shelf that she directed me to. She was pretty adamant in wanting me to deliver the message to you."

That was my mother's message? A title from a Dr. Seuss book sitting on my friend's shelf? After my epiphany from my father, I had hoped for something more profound. Was she trying to lecture me that I *should* consider myself lucky?

My friend reassured me that my mother's tone was "celebratory and loving." I thanked him. Perhaps Mom had rediscovered the sense of play she lost during her middle years. But what exactly did "lucky" mean?

Three years later, I had a dream in which my mother appeared to me. She no longer carried the worn-out look and weight of her later years. She appeared to be about 40 and was dressed in a long-sleeved blue top and matching capri pants, her hair loose and windswept. She waved with a big grin then darted off with friends, looking relaxed, pretty, and adventurous—free of family obligations. We didn't talk, but I was delighted for her new freedom.

When I was a child, my mother wanted me to be happy. But her desire felt less like a wish and more like a demand for me to hide my real feelings. I translated her intentions into "I want you to help me deal with my pain by being happy so that I will be happy. Please play it safe so that I don't have to feel my fear. And don't be sad, angry, or scared." But that mom from my childhood was gone, and now no one was asking me to deny or suppress complex feelings.

That morning, after the dream, I headed out, as usual, to take care of the horses. But as I mucked the paddock, I suddenly stopped. I turned toward the dawn, appreciating the stately row of Douglas firs on my neighbor's property as light began to fill the sky. Behind me, the stalls smelled of fresh hay. Above me, a crow flew on a cool wind, cawing with what sounded like delight.

I was hit with the realization that my mom's last message to me was right: I *was* lucky.

Mariah, my mare, nuzzled my cheek, and green hay drooled out of her mouth. She quietly stood as I threw my arms over her neck and sang "thank you" to her, to the property, to the life I was living, and to God. I was lucky—incredibly lucky—not just for the moment, but for the music playing in my head and for the right to be in this messy, beautiful, confused world.

I knew I would still have bad days when tragedy felt too heavy, aging seemed too burdensome, and the skies looked too gray. These came with the package of being human—an incredible gift that might not always feel like luck. But they would pass. No matter what, I could always return to the gratitude.

I stood still to absorb the blessing. Then, Mariah, with her eyes soft, cocked her ears and, as if knowing we were done, walked back to her stall and started munching her hay.

Wabi-Sabi

You are here on Earth so briefly. Spirit travels through your hands. Will your work be recognized? There is no guarantee. Yet, never forget what ignited it, the fierce call that invited you to be who you are. Let Beauty and Joy be your guides, and let love emerge from your creations.
—MARCO

During my time in Japan, I learned about the concept of *wabi-sabi*. This term is sometimes defined as "the perfection living within imperfection," though it also encapsulates the ideas of impermanence and simplicity. It is the flaw in the beam of a traditional Japanese house, elegant in its understated beauty. It is the ancient tea service bowl with its rough surfaces and irregularities that sits perfectly in the hand. It is the wilted tip on the camellia bloom placed in an ikebana arrangement, stunning in its simplicity.

On my land, I found wabi-sabi in the artful patterns of worm holes meandering through a rotting log and dramatic shadows cast on the caved-in roof of a neighbor's barn. Walking slowly, I discovered beauty in decay as well as in growth.

In my art, wabi-sabi meant embracing "mistakes" such as a stray mark on a drawing or an errant drop of paint on a sheet. Life did not have to be perfect to be wonderful, and neither did I.

The call of Spirit that was inspiring my life had nothing to do with "enlightenment" or its mundane younger siblings: "fixing myself" and "getting it right." It did not require me to transcend my flawed human condition. It *did* invite me to open more fully to the beauty around me and to embrace the world—and myself—with all of its and our collective imperfections, large and small.

As I let go of needing to fix myself, my pesky pack of gremlins—my inner judges—lost some of their influence. Yet, they too were part of my humanness. The more I was OK with myself "as is," the more I could I embrace my quirkiness—what my friend had once called "the clown in me." My personality, my nose, my searching, and my faith were uniquely mine. I didn't have to prove that the spiritual world existed or that my beloved Muses Isabel and Marco were real. These ideas, beliefs, and presences lived in the truth of my experience and within a universe filled with far more mystery than I could ever understand.

As I travel through the coming decades, I'll draw on my intuition, imagination, reason, and resilience. I hope to live with vulnerability, openness, joy, wonder, curiosity, and gratitude. I know I will stumble. And, in the spirit of wabi-sabi, that's fine. Each day becomes a reason to give thanks for the privilege of being alive, an opportunity to discover beauty and channel it into creative expression.

The voice that first propelled my journey stays with me:

There's more.

Only now, it has expanded:

There's STILL more.

And today, that *more* in its hugeness can be as simple as a dog's lick, a mare's nuzzle, or the gentle fragrance of peonies on a warm spring day.

A Blessing

*I*n the spirit of the Muses, I want to thank you and offer a blessing before we part:

May you feel the freedom to be imperfectly human and create—no longer needing to prove your worthiness.

May you find the deep story that lives within you and share it however you can.

May you put aside questions of talent and ask, "Where can I play? What brings me joy?"

May you befriend Beauty and notice how she lives both within you and around you.

May you bless your body, your senses, and the path they open to wonder.

May you cherish the spark that lies within.

May you feel grace, mystery, and connection.

May your heart stay open with gratitude.

May you have love—all you want—with times to give and times to receive.

As my father said, "It's all about the love."

And, when your body declines with age, may your Soul continue to deepen and your Spirit continue to soar.

Acknowledgments

Writing is a solitary pursuit, but I never felt alone on this journey. Thanks to the community who stood with me, which includes all of the people mentioned below as well as others I didn't have enough space or memory to mention but have nonetheless been pillars in my life and creative process.

First, the teachers: Jeffrey Davis' online book-writing program introduced me to a "pod" of committed writers—Juliet Bruce, Mindy Ohringer, and Carol Cannon—whose support was unwavering. Thanks to Christina Baldwin, who gave me permission to call myself a writer even when the evidence was scant, and the marvelous women I've met through her.

Thanks to Andy Couturier, a delightfully irreverent and supportive writing coach. Thanks, also, to Andy for introducing me to Bridget Lyons, my editor and behind-the-scenes star who anchored the book through months of revision. She balanced a dedication to craft and a supply of corrections, suggestions, and coaching with never-flagging encouragement. She was simply the best, helping me to steer clear of the potholes of self-judgment while turning editing into delight. I can't wait to start my next book so I can work with her again!

I promised my early readers Claire Bronson, Carol Cannon, Liz Monroe-Cook, Angelique Electra, and Rondi Lightmark that there would be a special place in heaven for anyone willing to read a first draft that was so far from its future self. Thanks to all the advanced readers who blessed me with their endorsements for this much-improved version.

Carla Pryne and Stephen Silha were both pillars of support and advocates for the book and for my fundraising, helping me to do what

I barely had the courage to do. Thanks, in turn, to all the donors, too many to list, who surprised me, delighted me, and confirmed that writing a book truly is a community venture.

Thanks to my "Story Group" and other Yale colleagues who reentered my life almost 40 years after we were together in graduate school. As we shared our stories, we discovered and nurtured connections often deeper than those from our younger days. My sisters in "The Gathering," a group that has been convening yearly for the past 35 years, warrant thanks for supporting my metamorphosis from a self-doubting consultant to a wiser, truer version of myself. They taught me so much about what aging into our better selves can look like.

I am grateful for creative inspiration from Richard Geer and Story Bridge, Chloë Goodchild and her Naked Voice community, and artists Geri Peterson, Nicholas Wilton, Heather Williams, Bruce Morser, and Dana Lynne Andersen. Much gratitude and love to my voice teacher and spiritual mentor, Peggy Norcross, whom I continue to miss many years after her passing.

David and Julia Spangler and the Lorian Community continue to teach me about being fully myself and tapping into spiritual wisdom as I walk this Earth. (The Muses felt comfortable around them!) Thanks to Beverly Burns, my dear longtime friend, for introducing me to the work of Rudolf Steiner many years ago.

Everyone who read my blog over the past eight years has made me a better writer as I've worked each week to create posts worthy of their attention. My friends who have heard about and supported "the book" for many years deserve boundless thanks for their patience; perhaps I'll grow conversational and see them again soon! Lots of love and thanks to my extended family. They were always precious to me, but they have become even more so as I age.

As the book moved toward publishing and production, the team at 1106 Design guided me skillfully along the way. Thanks to Michele

DeFillipo and Ronda Rawlins for their professionalism and attention to detail.

A huge thanks and place in my heart goes to Lorilyn Parmer Folks, a fellow misfit from business school who shares my passion for creativity. For 40 years, we have coached each other on our mutual quests to live creative, soul-filled lives. She helped midwife the process of bringing forth this book through her writerly suggestions and ability to throw me an occasional lifeline. I couldn't have done it without her. May all creatives have such a committed partner!

And, of course, thanks to the subtle stars, the Muses, and any other unseen advisors who guided this book.

To Steve Brown, whom I lovingly call "my rock," my biggest thanks. Steve is the foundation for most everything in my life and an unwavering advocate for all of my creative work, including this book. He also helps care of "the boys," Winston and Royce, who bring both muddy paws and constant joy into our lives.

Finally, my sister inspired me with her courage in the face of great adversity. This book is dedicated to her. May the love within it support her transition to the spirit realm.

About the Author

*S*ally Jean Fox, PhD, is a writer, coach, performer, and artist. As head of Engaging Presence, she has coached hundreds of professionals to design their lives around what matters most to them and share their stories. She also supports clients to nurture their inner spark and design lives that support their creative aspirations.

Sally writes regularly for *3rd Act Magazine, Medium,* the website *60 and Me,* and *Substack,* and produces the *Vital Presence* podcast. Find her weekly blog at EngagingPresence.com.

In her earlier career, Sally directed pioneering leadership programs aimed at fostering self-awareness, presence and meaningful engagement with others. She was the founding director of the Graduate Management Program at Antioch University Seattle. She holds a PhD from the Fielding Graduate University, an MBA from Yale University, and an MA from the University of Michigan.

She lives with her husband on an island near Seattle where you may find her writing, weeding, riding her Connemara mare, or enjoying their twin springer spaniels, the "joy boys."

She'd love to hear about your discoveries about aging and the creative life. You can reach her at www. meetingthemuseaftermidlife.com where you can find additional resources and practices to help you live your most creative life.

Printed in Great Britain
by Amazon

34338180R00180